MW01114092

Risks Dashboard
Complete Self-Assessment Guide

The guidance in this Self-Assessment is based on Risks Dashboard best practices and standards in business process architecture, design and quality management. The guidance is also based on the professional judgment of the individual collaborators listed in the Acknowledgments.

Notice of rights

Trademarks

Table of Contents

About The Art of Service

The Art of Service, Business Process Architects since 2000, is dedicated to helping stakeholders achieve excellence.

Defining, designing, creating, and implementing a process to solve a stakeholders challenge or meet an objective is the most valuable role... In EVERY group, company, organization and department.

Unless you're talking a one-time, single-use project, there should be a process. Whether that process is managed and implemented by humans, AI, or a combination of the two, it needs to be designed by someone with a complex enough perspective to ask the right questions.

Someone capable of asking the right questions and step back and say, 'What are we really trying to accomplish here? And is there a different way to look at it?'

With The Art of Service's Standard Requirements Self-Assessments, we empower people who can do just that — whether their title is marketer, entrepreneur, manager, salesperson, consultant, Business Process Manager, executive assistant, IT Manager, CIO etc... —they are the people who rule the future. They are people who watch the process as it happens, and ask the right questions to make the process work better.

Contact us when you need any support with this Self-Assessment and any help with templates, blue-prints and examples of standard documents you might need:

http://theartofservice.com
service@theartofservice.com

Included Resources - how to access

Included with your purchase of the book is the Risks Dashboard

Self-Assessment Spreadsheet Dashboard which contains all questions and Self-Assessment areas and auto-generates insights, graphs, and project RACI planning - all with examples to get you started right away.

How? Simply send an email to
access@theartofservice.com
with this books' title in the subject to get the Risks Dashboard Self Assessment Tool right away.

You will receive the following contents with New and Updated specific criteria:

• The latest quick edition of the book in PDF

• The latest complete edition of the book in PDF, which criteria correspond to the criteria in...

• The Self-Assessment Excel Dashboard, and...

• Example pre-filled Self-Assessment Excel Dashboard to get familiar with results generation

• In-depth specific Checklists covering the topic

• Project management checklists and templates to assist with implementation

INCLUDES LIFETIME SELF ASSESSMENT UPDATES

Every self assessment comes with Lifetime Updates and Lifetime Free Updated Books. Lifetime Updates is an industry-first feature which allows you to receive verified self assessment updates, ensuring you always have the most accurate information at your fingertips.

Get it now- you will be glad you did - do it now, before you forget.

Send an email to **access@theartofservice.com** with this books' title in the subject to get the Risks Dashboard Self Assessment Tool right away.

Purpose of this Self-Assessment

This Self-Assessment has been developed to improve understanding of the requirements and elements of Risks Dashboard, based on best practices and standards in business process architecture, design and quality management.

It is designed to allow for a rapid Self-Assessment to determine how closely existing management practices and procedures correspond to the elements of the Self-Assessment.

The criteria of requirements and elements of Risks Dashboard have been rephrased in the format of a Self-Assessment questionnaire, with a seven-criterion scoring system, as explained in this document.

In this format, even with limited background knowledge of Risks Dashboard, a manager can quickly review existing operations to determine how they measure up to the standards. This in turn can serve as the starting point of a 'gap analysis' to identify management tools or system elements that might usefully be implemented in the organization to help improve overall performance.

How to use the Self-Assessment

On the following pages are a series of questions to identify to what extent your Risks Dashboard initiative is complete in comparison to the requirements set in standards.

To facilitate answering the questions, there is a space in front of each question to enter a score on a scale of '1' to '5'.

1 Strongly Disagree

2 Disagree

3 Neutral

4 Agree

5 Strongly Agree

Read the question and rate it with the following in front of mind:

'In my belief, the answer to this question is clearly defined'.

There are two ways in which you can choose to interpret this statement;
1. how aware are you that the answer to the question is clearly defined
2. for more in-depth analysis you can choose to gather evidence and confirm the answer to the question. This obviously will take more time, most Self-Assessment users opt for the first way to interpret the question and dig deeper later on based on the outcome of the overall Self-Assessment.

A score of '1' would mean that the answer is not clear at all, where a '5' would mean the answer is crystal clear and defined. Leave emtpy when the question is not applicable or you don't want to answer it, you can skip it without affecting your score. Write your score in the space provided.

After you have responded to all the appropriate statements in each section, compute your average score for that section, using the formula provided, and round to the nearest tenth. Then transfer to the corresponding spoke in the Risks Dashboard Scorecard on the second next page of the Self-Assessment.

Your completed Risks Dashboard Scorecard will give you a clear presentation of which Risks Dashboard areas need attention.

Risks Dashboard
Scorecard Example

Example of how the finalized Scorecard can look like:

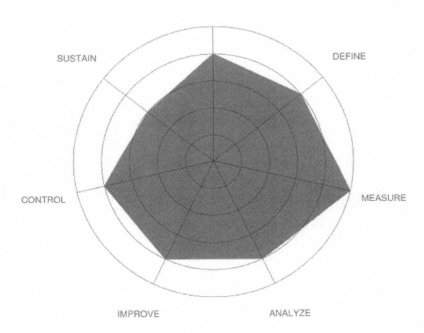

Risks Dashboard
Scorecard

Your Scores:

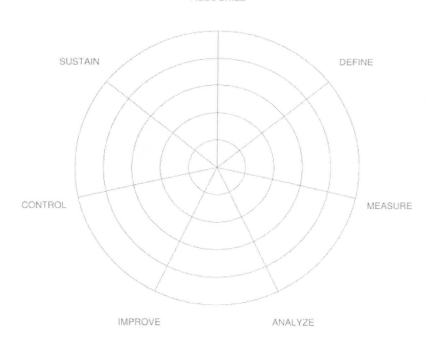

BEGINNING OF THE SELF-ASSESSMENT:

CRITERION #1: RECOGNIZE

INTENT: Be aware of the need for change. Recognize that there is an unfavorable variation, problem or symptom.

In my belief, the answer to this question is clearly defined:

5 Strongly Agree

4 Agree

3 Neutral

2 Disagree

1 Strongly Disagree

1. What is the problem and/or vulnerability?
<--- Score

2. How do you identify the kinds of information that you will need?
<--- Score

3. Do you need different information or graphics?
<--- Score

4. Will a response program recognize when a crisis occurs and provide some level of response?
<--- Score

5. What are the expected benefits of Risks Dashboard to the stakeholder?
<--- Score

6. What situation(s) led to this Risks Dashboard Self Assessment?
<--- Score

7. How many trainings, in total, are needed?
<--- Score

8. What are the minority interests and what amount of minority interests can be recognized?
<--- Score

9. How does it fit into your organizational needs and tasks?
<--- Score

10. Who needs what information?
<--- Score

11. Who needs budgets?
<--- Score

12. Who should resolve the Risks Dashboard issues?
<--- Score

13. What Risks Dashboard capabilities do you need?
<--- Score

14. To what extent does each concerned units management team recognize Risks Dashboard as an effective investment?

<--- Score

15. What tools and technologies are needed for a custom Risks Dashboard project?

<--- Score

16. How do you recognize an Risks Dashboard objection?

<--- Score

17. What are the Risks Dashboard resources needed?

<--- Score

18. Are your goals realistic? Do you need to redefine your problem? Perhaps the problem has changed or maybe you have reached your goal and need to set a new one?

<--- Score

19. What Risks Dashboard problem should be solved?

<--- Score

20. What is the smallest subset of the problem you can usefully solve?

<--- Score

21. Why is this needed?

<--- Score

22. Why the need?

<--- Score

23. How do you assess your Risks Dashboard workforce capability and capacity needs, including skills, competencies, and staffing levels?
<--- Score

24. What are the stakeholder objectives to be achieved with Risks Dashboard?
<--- Score

25. How are you going to measure success?
<--- Score

26. Can management personnel recognize the monetary benefit of Risks Dashboard?
<--- Score

27. What activities does the governance board need to consider?
<--- Score

28. What is the extent or complexity of the Risks Dashboard problem?
<--- Score

29. Are there Risks Dashboard problems defined?
<--- Score

30. Which information does the Risks Dashboard business case need to include?
<--- Score

31. What is the problem or issue?
<--- Score

32. What needs to stay?

<--- Score

33. What problems are you facing and how do you consider Risks Dashboard will circumvent those obstacles?
<--- Score

34. Does Risks Dashboard create potential expectations in other areas that need to be recognized and considered?
<--- Score

35. What prevents you from making the changes you know will make you a more effective Risks Dashboard leader?
<--- Score

36. Do you need to avoid or amend any Risks Dashboard activities?
<--- Score

37. Which issues are too important to ignore?
<--- Score

38. How much are sponsors, customers, partners, stakeholders involved in Risks Dashboard? In other words, what are the risks, if Risks Dashboard does not deliver successfully?
<--- Score

39. Looking at each person individually – does every one have the qualities which are needed to work in this group?
<--- Score

40. What Risks Dashboard coordination do you

need?
<--- Score

41. Are employees recognized or rewarded for performance that demonstrates the highest levels of integrity?
<--- Score

42. Are there any specific expectations or concerns about the Risks Dashboard team, Risks Dashboard itself?
<--- Score

43. What would happen if Risks Dashboard weren't done?
<--- Score

44. To what extent would your organization benefit from being recognized as a award recipient?
<--- Score

45. Are you dealing with any of the same issues today as yesterday? What can you do about this?
<--- Score

46. Who needs to know about Risks Dashboard?
<--- Score

47. Does the problem have ethical dimensions?
<--- Score

48. Who else hopes to benefit from it?
<--- Score

49. Are there regulatory / compliance issues?
<--- Score

50. Would you recognize a threat from the inside?
<--- Score

51. Will it solve real problems?
<--- Score

52. As a sponsor, customer or management, how important is it to meet goals, objectives?
<--- Score

53. Which needs are not included or involved?
<--- Score

54. Are controls defined to recognize and contain problems?
<--- Score

55. Think about the people you identified for your Risks Dashboard project and the project responsibilities you would assign to them, what kind of training do you think they would need to perform these responsibilities effectively?
<--- Score

56. What are your needs in relation to Risks Dashboard skills, labor, equipment, and markets?
<--- Score

57. When a Risks Dashboard manager recognizes a problem, what options are available?
<--- Score

58. What vendors make products that address the Risks Dashboard needs?
<--- Score

59. What do employees need in the short term?
<--- Score

60. Whom do you really need or want to serve?
<--- Score

61. What resources or support might you need?
<--- Score

62. Are problem definition and motivation clearly presented?
<--- Score

63. Are there recognized Risks Dashboard problems?
<--- Score

64. Do you know what you need to know about Risks Dashboard?
<--- Score

65. How are training requirements identified?
<--- Score

66. What does Risks Dashboard success mean to the stakeholders?
<--- Score

67. How do you identify subcontractor relationships?
<--- Score

68. Are employees recognized for desired behaviors?
<--- Score

69. How are the Risks Dashboard's objectives aligned

to the group's overall stakeholder strategy?
<--- Score

70. What creative shifts do you need to take?
<--- Score

71. Will new equipment/products be required to facilitate Risks Dashboard delivery, for example is new software needed?
<--- Score

72. Will Risks Dashboard deliverables need to be tested and, if so, by whom?
<--- Score

73. What are the timeframes required to resolve each of the issues/problems?
<--- Score

74. What are the clients issues and concerns?
<--- Score

75. Is it clear when you think of the day ahead of you what activities and tasks you need to complete?
<--- Score

76. Do you have/need 24-hour access to key personnel?
<--- Score

77. Is the need for organizational change recognized?
<--- Score

78. What needs to be done?
<--- Score

79. How do you recognize an objection?
<--- Score

80. What do you need to start doing?
<--- Score

81. What is the recognized need?
<--- Score

82. How do you take a forward-looking perspective in identifying Risks Dashboard research related to market response and models?
<--- Score

83. What extra resources will you need?
<--- Score

84. Does your organization need more Risks Dashboard education?
<--- Score

85. What Risks Dashboard events should you attend?
<--- Score

86. What training and capacity building actions are needed to implement proposed reforms?
<--- Score

87. Is it needed?
<--- Score

88. Did you miss any major Risks Dashboard issues?
<--- Score

89. Who defines the rules in relation to any given

issue?

<--- Score

90. Is the quality assurance team identified?

<--- Score

91. Are there any revenue recognition issues?

<--- Score

92. How can auditing be a preventative security measure?

<--- Score

93. For your Risks Dashboard project, identify and describe the business environment, is there more than one layer to the business environment?

<--- Score

94. Who are your key stakeholders who need to sign off?

<--- Score

Add up total points for this section:

_ _ _ _ _ = Total points for this section

Divided by: _ _ _ _ _ _ (number of statements answered) = _ _ _ _ _ _
Average score for this section

Transfer your score to the Risks Dashboard Index at the beginning of the Self-Assessment.

CRITERION #2: DEFINE:

INTENT: Formulate the stakeholder problem. Define the problem, needs and objectives.

In my belief, the answer to this question is clearly defined:

5 Strongly Agree

4 Agree

3 Neutral

2 Disagree

1 Strongly Disagree

1. What sources do you use to gather information for a Risks Dashboard study?
<--- Score

2. Are accountability and ownership for Risks Dashboard clearly defined?
<--- Score

3. Are required metrics defined, what are they?

<--- Score

4. Who is gathering Risks Dashboard information?
<--- Score

5. How often are the team meetings?
<--- Score

6. What are the Roles and Responsibilities for each team member and its leadership? Where is this documented?
<--- Score

7. Is the Risks Dashboard scope manageable?
<--- Score

8. What are the Risks Dashboard use cases?
<--- Score

9. When is the estimated completion date?
<--- Score

10. When are meeting minutes sent out? Who is on the distribution list?
<--- Score

11. What is out-of-scope initially?
<--- Score

12. Has the Risks Dashboard work been fairly and/or equitably divided and delegated among team members who are qualified and capable to perform the work? Has everyone contributed?
<--- Score

13. Has a team charter been developed and

communicated?
<--- Score

14. Is there a Risks Dashboard management
charter, including stakeholder case, problem and
goal statements, scope, milestones, roles and
responsibilities, communication plan?
<--- Score

15. Is Risks Dashboard linked to key stakeholder goals
and objectives?
<--- Score

16. Is there a completed, verified, and validated high-
level 'as is' (not 'should be' or 'could be') stakeholder
process map?
<--- Score

17. What constraints exist that might impact the
team?
<--- Score

18. How do you manage scope?
<--- Score

19. Do you all define Risks Dashboard in the same
way?
<--- Score

**20. Is special Risks Dashboard user knowledge
required?**
<--- Score

21. Has your scope been defined?
<--- Score

22. Who are the Risks Dashboard improvement team members, including Management Leads and Coaches?
<--- Score

23. What is the context?
<--- Score

24. Do you have a Risks Dashboard success story or case study ready to tell and share?
<--- Score

25. What would be the goal or target for a Risks Dashboard's improvement team?
<--- Score

26. Who is gathering information?
<--- Score

27. Has a project plan, Gantt chart, or similar been developed/completed?
<--- Score

28. What system do you use for gathering Risks Dashboard information?
<--- Score

29. Have the customer needs been translated into specific, measurable requirements? How?
<--- Score

30. Has the direction changed at all during the course of Risks Dashboard? If so, when did it change and why?
<--- Score

31. Has the improvement team collected the 'voice of the customer' (obtained feedback – qualitative and quantitative)?
<--- Score

32. Are audit criteria, scope, frequency and methods defined?
<--- Score

33. How do you hand over Risks Dashboard context?
<--- Score

34. Has everyone on the team, including the team leaders, been properly trained?
<--- Score

35. What is the worst case scenario?
<--- Score

36. What is the scope of the Risks Dashboard work?
<--- Score

37. How do you manage changes in Risks Dashboard requirements?
<--- Score

38. Are resources adequate for the scope?
<--- Score

39. How do you gather requirements?
<--- Score

40. What information do you gather?
<--- Score

41. What are the rough order estimates on cost savings/opportunities that Risks Dashboard brings?
<--- Score

42. How is the team tracking and documenting its work?
<--- Score

43. What is out of scope?
<--- Score

44. Has a Risks Dashboard requirement not been met?
<--- Score

45. How will the Risks Dashboard team and the group measure complete success of Risks Dashboard?
<--- Score

46. How would you define Risks Dashboard leadership?
<--- Score

47. How do you keep key subject matter experts in the loop?
<--- Score

48. Do you have organizational privacy requirements?
<--- Score

49. Has a high-level 'as is' process map been completed, verified and validated?
<--- Score

50. Are there any constraints known that bear on the ability to perform Risks Dashboard work? How is the team addressing them?

<--- Score

51. What baselines are required to be defined and managed?
<--- Score

52. Is the team adequately staffed with the desired cross-functionality? If not, what additional resources are available to the team?
<--- Score

53. What is the definition of success?
<--- Score

54. What information should you gather?
<--- Score

55. How do you gather Risks Dashboard requirements?
<--- Score

56. Does the team have regular meetings?
<--- Score

57. What was the context?
<--- Score

58. How and when will the baselines be defined?
<--- Score

59. Is the team equipped with available and reliable resources?
<--- Score

60. The political context: who holds power?
<--- Score

61. Is scope creep really all bad news?
<--- Score

62. Is there any additional Risks Dashboard definition of success?
<--- Score

63. What is in scope?
<--- Score

64. What customer feedback methods were used to solicit their input?
<--- Score

65. Is the current 'as is' process being followed? If not, what are the discrepancies?
<--- Score

66. What are the tasks and definitions?
<--- Score

67. Is the work to date meeting requirements?
<--- Score

68. How can the value of Risks Dashboard be defined?
<--- Score

69. Is there a critical path to deliver Risks Dashboard results?
<--- Score

70. Has/have the customer(s) been identified?
<--- Score

71. How would you define the culture at your organization, how susceptible is it to Risks Dashboard changes?
<--- Score

72. What Risks Dashboard services do you require?
<--- Score

73. Is data collected and displayed to better understand customer(s) critical needs and requirements.
<--- Score

74. Is the Risks Dashboard scope complete and appropriately sized?
<--- Score

75. What is the scope?
<--- Score

76. Are roles and responsibilities formally defined?
<--- Score

77. What is a worst-case scenario for losses?
<--- Score

78. Does the scope remain the same?
<--- Score

79. What scope do you want your strategy to cover?
<--- Score

80. Have all basic functions of Risks Dashboard been defined?
<--- Score

81. How do you gather the stories?
<--- Score

82. How did the Risks Dashboard manager receive input to the development of a Risks Dashboard improvement plan and the estimated completion dates/times of each activity?
<--- Score

83. What are the requirements for audit information?
<--- Score

84. How was the 'as is' process map developed, reviewed, verified and validated?
<--- Score

85. How does the Risks Dashboard manager ensure against scope creep?
<--- Score

86. What gets examined?
<--- Score

87. What key stakeholder process output measure(s) does Risks Dashboard leverage and how?
<--- Score

88. When is/was the Risks Dashboard start date?
<--- Score

89. What critical content must be communicated – who, what, when, where, and how?
<--- Score

90. What is the scope of Risks Dashboard?

<--- Score

91. What are the record-keeping requirements of Risks Dashboard activities?
<--- Score

92. What Risks Dashboard requirements should be gathered?
<--- Score

93. Are the Risks Dashboard requirements testable?
<--- Score

94. Who defines (or who defined) the rules and roles?
<--- Score

95. How have you defined all Risks Dashboard requirements first?
<--- Score

96. Is the improvement team aware of the different versions of a process: what they think it is vs. what it actually is vs. what it should be vs. what it could be?
<--- Score

97. What scope to assess?
<--- Score

98. How do you catch Risks Dashboard definition inconsistencies?
<--- Score

99. What specifically is the problem? Where does it occur? When does it occur? What is its extent?
<--- Score

100. Do the problem and goal statements meet the SMART criteria (specific, measurable, attainable, relevant, and time-bound)?
<--- Score

101. Is Risks Dashboard currently on schedule according to the plan?
<--- Score

102. What are the boundaries of the scope? What is in bounds and what is not? What is the start point? What is the stop point?
<--- Score

103. Have all of the relationships been defined properly?
<--- Score

104. What defines best in class?
<--- Score

105. Where can you gather more information?
<--- Score

106. If substitutes have been appointed, have they been briefed on the Risks Dashboard goals and received regular communications as to the progress to date?
<--- Score

107. Are there different segments of customers?
<--- Score

108. Are different versions of process maps needed to account for the different types of inputs?
<--- Score

109. Has anyone else (internal or external to the group) attempted to solve this problem or a similar one before? If so, what knowledge can be leveraged from these previous efforts?
<--- Score

110. What is in the scope and what is not in scope?
<--- Score

111. Have specific policy objectives been defined?
<--- Score

112. Are approval levels defined for contracts and supplements to contracts?
<--- Score

113. What are the compelling stakeholder reasons for embarking on Risks Dashboard?
<--- Score

114. What happens if Risks Dashboard's scope changes?
<--- Score

115. What are the dynamics of the communication plan?
<--- Score

116. How do you think the partners involved in Risks Dashboard would have defined success?
<--- Score

117. Are customer(s) identified and segmented according to their different needs and requirements?
<--- Score

118. What is the definition of Risks Dashboard excellence?
<--- Score

119. Scope of sensitive information?
<--- Score

120. Is there regularly 100% attendance at the team meetings? If not, have appointed substitutes attended to preserve cross-functionality and full representation?
<--- Score

121. In what way can you redefine the criteria of choice clients have in your category in your favor?
<--- Score

122. Who approved the Risks Dashboard scope?
<--- Score

123. What is the scope of the Risks Dashboard effort?
<--- Score

124. Is it clearly defined in and to your organization what you do?
<--- Score

125. How will variation in the actual durations of each activity be dealt with to ensure that the expected Risks Dashboard results are met?
<--- Score

126. What are the core elements of the Risks Dashboard business case?
<--- Score

127. What are (control) requirements for Risks Dashboard Information?

<--- Score

128. Is there a completed SIPOC representation, describing the Suppliers, Inputs, Process, Outputs, and Customers?

<--- Score

129. How are consistent Risks Dashboard definitions important?

<--- Score

130. What intelligence can you gather?

<--- Score

131. Is the scope of Risks Dashboard defined?

<--- Score

132. What knowledge or experience is required?

<--- Score

133. Are all requirements met?

<--- Score

Add up total points for this section:
_ _ _ _ _ = Total points for this section

Divided by: _ _ _ _ _ _ (number of statements answered) = _ _ _ _ _ _
Average score for this section

Transfer your score to the Risks Dashboard Index at the beginning of the Self-Assessment.

CRITERION #3: MEASURE:

INTENT: Gather the correct data.
Measure the current performance and
evolution of the situation.

In my belief, the answer to this
question is clearly defined:

5 Strongly Agree

4 Agree

3 Neutral

2 Disagree

1 Strongly Disagree

1. How do you verify Risks Dashboard completeness
and accuracy?
<--- Score

2. What are the current costs of the Risks Dashboard
process?
<--- Score

3. Are Risks Dashboard vulnerabilities categorized

and prioritized?
<--- Score

4. How do you measure efficient delivery of Risks Dashboard services?
<--- Score

5. Are supply costs steady or fluctuating?
<--- Score

6. What is your Risks Dashboard quality cost segregation study?
<--- Score

7. What details are required of the Risks Dashboard cost structure?
<--- Score

8. What is measured? Why?
<--- Score

9. Who should receive measurement reports?
<--- Score

10. Are there measurements based on task performance?
<--- Score

11. How do you measure success?
<--- Score

12. When a disaster occurs, who gets priority?
<--- Score

13. How do you verify performance?
<--- Score

14. How will costs be allocated?
<--- Score

15. How will your organization measure success?
<--- Score

16. How is progress measured?
<--- Score

17. What disadvantage does this cause for the user?
<--- Score

18. What are the Risks Dashboard key cost drivers?
<--- Score

19. How will effects be measured?
<--- Score

20. Is there an opportunity to verify requirements?
<--- Score

21. When should you bother with diagrams?
<--- Score

22. How do you control the overall costs of your work processes?
<--- Score

23. What is an unallowable cost?
<--- Score

24. What causes extra work or rework?
<--- Score

25. Does management have the right priorities

among projects?
<--- Score

26. What measurements are possible, practicable and meaningful?
<--- Score

27. How do you quantify and qualify impacts?
<--- Score

28. What is the cause of any Risks Dashboard gaps?
<--- Score

29. Are you able to realize any cost savings?
<--- Score

30. Do you aggressively reward and promote the people who have the biggest impact on creating excellent Risks Dashboard services/products?
<--- Score

31. Have you made assumptions about the shape of the future, particularly its impact on your customers and competitors?
<--- Score

32. What does your operating model cost?
<--- Score

33. What are the costs?
<--- Score

34. What causes innovation to fail or succeed in your organization?
<--- Score

35. What can be used to verify compliance?
<--- Score

36. What are the uncertainties surrounding estimates of impact?
<--- Score

37. Did you tackle the cause or the symptom?
<--- Score

38. Are actual costs in line with budgeted costs?
<--- Score

39. Who is involved in verifying compliance?
<--- Score

40. What are your key Risks Dashboard organizational performance measures, including key short and longer-term financial measures?
<--- Score

41. How do you verify your resources?
<--- Score

42. Will Risks Dashboard have an impact on current business continuity, disaster recovery processes and/or infrastructure?
<--- Score

43. How do you prevent mis-estimating cost?
<--- Score

44. How are costs allocated?
<--- Score

45. What are your customers expectations and measures?

<--- Score

46. Which measures and indicators matter?

<--- Score

47. Where can you go to verify the info?

<--- Score

48. What are the costs of delaying Risks Dashboard action?

<--- Score

49. What could cause you to change course?

<--- Score

50. What are the operational costs after Risks Dashboard deployment?

<--- Score

51. Are missed Risks Dashboard opportunities costing your organization money?

<--- Score

52. What is your decision requirements diagram?

<--- Score

53. How sensitive must the Risks Dashboard strategy be to cost?

<--- Score

54. Does a Risks Dashboard quantification method exist?

<--- Score

55. Are there any easy-to-implement alternatives to Risks Dashboard? Sometimes other solutions are available that do not require the cost implications of a full-blown project?

<--- Score

56. Do you effectively measure and reward individual and team performance?

<--- Score

57. Are indirect costs charged to the Risks Dashboard program?

<--- Score

58. Have design-to-cost goals been established?

<--- Score

59. Which costs should be taken into account?

<--- Score

60. What could cause delays in the schedule?

<--- Score

61. What are the Risks Dashboard investment costs?

<--- Score

62. What do people want to verify?

<--- Score

63. Have you included everything in your Risks Dashboard cost models?

<--- Score

64. What drives O&M cost?

<--- Score

65. What are your primary costs, revenues, assets?
<--- Score

66. What are the types and number of measures to use?
<--- Score

67. What relevant entities could be measured?
<--- Score

68. Is the solution cost-effective?
<--- Score

69. Where is the cost?
<--- Score

70. Do the benefits outweigh the costs?
<--- Score

71. When are costs are incurred?
<--- Score

72. What do you measure and why?
<--- Score

73. How do you measure lifecycle phases?
<--- Score

74. How will you measure success?
<--- Score

75. What happens if cost savings do not materialize?
<--- Score

76. How can a Risks Dashboard test verify your ideas

or assumptions?
<--- Score

77. Which Risks Dashboard impacts are significant?
<--- Score

78. What would be a real cause for concern?
<--- Score

79. Why do the measurements/indicators matter?
<--- Score

80. Do you have an issue in getting priority?
<--- Score

81. How is performance measured?
<--- Score

82. How do you verify if Risks Dashboard is built right?
<--- Score

83. What harm might be caused?
<--- Score

84. Are there competing Risks Dashboard priorities?
<--- Score

85. How can you reduce the costs of obtaining inputs?
<--- Score

86. What is the Risks Dashboard business impact?
<--- Score

87. Do you have a flow diagram of what happens?
<--- Score

88. How frequently do you track Risks Dashboard measures?
<--- Score

89. Is it possible to estimate the impact of unanticipated complexity such as wrong or failed assumptions, feedback, etcetera on proposed reforms?
<--- Score

90. What are the strategic priorities for this year?
<--- Score

91. What are your operating costs?
<--- Score

92. What is the total fixed cost?
<--- Score

93. What does losing customers cost your organization?
<--- Score

94. At what cost?
<--- Score

95. What are you verifying?
<--- Score

96. How long to keep data and how to manage retention costs?
<--- Score

97. How do you aggregate measures across priorities?
<--- Score

98. How do you verify and validate the Risks Dashboard data?
<--- Score

99. Are the units of measure consistent?
<--- Score

100. What evidence is there and what is measured?
<--- Score

101. Where is it measured?
<--- Score

102. How do your measurements capture actionable Risks Dashboard information for use in exceeding your customers expectations and securing your customers engagement?
<--- Score

103. What is the root cause(s) of the problem?
<--- Score

104. How can you measure the performance?
<--- Score

105. What does verifying compliance entail?
<--- Score

106. Was a business case (cost/benefit) developed?
<--- Score

107. Are you aware of what could cause a problem?
<--- Score

108. What measurements are being captured?
<--- Score

109. How will success or failure be measured?
<--- Score

110. What are the costs of reform?
<--- Score

111. What users will be impacted?
<--- Score

112. How will measures be used to manage and adapt?
<--- Score

113. What is the total cost related to deploying Risks Dashboard, including any consulting or professional services?
<--- Score

114. What are hidden Risks Dashboard quality costs?
<--- Score

115. What methods are feasible and acceptable to estimate the impact of reforms?
<--- Score

116. What does a Test Case verify?
<--- Score

117. Are you taking your company in the direction of better and revenue or cheaper and cost?
<--- Score

118. How are measurements made?

<--- Score

119. What are the estimated costs of proposed changes?

<--- Score

120. What potential environmental factors impact the Risks Dashboard effort?

<--- Score

121. How much does it cost?

<--- Score

122. Are the Risks Dashboard benefits worth its costs?

<--- Score

123. How can you manage cost down?

<--- Score

124. Among the Risks Dashboard product and service cost to be estimated, which is considered hardest to estimate?

<--- Score

125. Has a cost center been established?

<--- Score

126. What causes investor action?

<--- Score

127. How can you measure Risks Dashboard in a systematic way?

<--- Score

128. Who pays the cost?

<--- Score

129. Does the Risks Dashboard task fit the client's priorities?
<--- Score

130. What would it cost to replace your technology?
<--- Score

131. What causes mismanagement?
<--- Score

132. How do you verify the authenticity of the data and information used?
<--- Score

133. How can you reduce costs?
<--- Score

134. What tests verify requirements?
<--- Score

135. Is the cost worth the Risks Dashboard effort ?
<--- Score

136. How frequently do you verify your Risks Dashboard strategy?
<--- Score

137. How do you verify the Risks Dashboard requirements quality?
<--- Score

138. Do you verify that corrective actions were taken?
<--- Score

139. Do you have any cost Risks Dashboard limitation requirements?

<--- Score

140. How are you verifying it?

<--- Score

141. What is the cost of rework?

<--- Score

142. How will you measure your Risks Dashboard effectiveness?

<--- Score

Add up total points for this section:

_____ = Total points for this section

Divided by: _____ (number of statements answered) = _____ Average score for this section

Transfer your score to the Risks Dashboard Index at the beginning of the Self-Assessment.

CRITERION #4: ANALYZE:

INTENT: Analyze causes, assumptions
and hypotheses.

In my belief, the answer to this
question is clearly defined:

5 Strongly Agree

4 Agree

3 Neutral

2 Disagree

1 Strongly Disagree

1. Who gets your output?
<--- Score

2. How difficult is it to qualify what Risks Dashboard
ROI is?
<--- Score

**3. How do you use Risks Dashboard data and
information to support organizational decision
making and innovation?**

<--- Score

4. What internal processes need improvement?
<--- Score

5. How do you define collaboration and team output?
<--- Score

6. What qualifications do Risks Dashboard leaders need?
<--- Score

7. What data is gathered?
<--- Score

8. What were the crucial 'moments of truth' on the process map?
<--- Score

9. Was a detailed process map created to amplify critical steps of the 'as is' stakeholder process?
<--- Score

10. When should a process be art not science?
<--- Score

11. Is the performance gap determined?
<--- Score

12. How will the change process be managed?
<--- Score

13. What qualifications and skills do you need?
<--- Score

14. Who qualifies to gain access to data?

<--- Score

15. What information qualified as important?
<--- Score

16. Think about some of the processes you undertake within your organization, which do you own?
<--- Score

17. A compounding model resolution with available relevant data can often provide insight towards a solution methodology; which Risks Dashboard models, tools and techniques are necessary?
<--- Score

18. How do you promote understanding that opportunity for improvement is not criticism of the status quo, or the people who created the status quo?
<--- Score

19. What training and qualifications will you need?
<--- Score

20. What types of data do your Risks Dashboard indicators require?
<--- Score

21. What are your key performance measures or indicators and in-process measures for the control and improvement of your Risks Dashboard processes?
<--- Score

22. What are your current levels and trends in key measures or indicators of Risks Dashboard product

and process performance that are important to and directly serve your customers? How do these results compare with the performance of your competitors and other organizations with similar offerings?
<--- Score

23. What is your organizations system for selecting qualified vendors?
<--- Score

24. How many input/output points does it require?
<--- Score

25. What are the processes for audit reporting and management?
<--- Score

26. Were there any improvement opportunities identified from the process analysis?
<--- Score

27. What kind of crime could a potential new hire have committed that would not only not disqualify him/her from being hired by your organization, but would actually indicate that he/she might be a particularly good fit?
<--- Score

28. Record-keeping requirements flow from the records needed as inputs, outputs, controls and for transformation of a Risks Dashboard process, are the records needed as inputs to the Risks Dashboard process available?
<--- Score

29. Can you add value to the current Risks Dashboard

decision-making process (largely qualitative) by incorporating uncertainty modeling (more quantitative)?
<--- Score

30. Are you missing Risks Dashboard opportunities?
<--- Score

31. What conclusions were drawn from the team's data collection and analysis? How did the team reach these conclusions?
<--- Score

32. How will corresponding data be collected?
<--- Score

33. Are Risks Dashboard changes recognized early enough to be approved through the regular process?
<--- Score

34. How has the Risks Dashboard data been gathered?
<--- Score

35. What process improvements will be needed?
<--- Score

36. Where is the data coming from to measure compliance?
<--- Score

37. How often will data be collected for measures?
<--- Score

38. What do you need to qualify?
<--- Score

39. How is data used for program management and improvement?
<--- Score

40. Who will facilitate the team and process?
<--- Score

41. What are evaluation criteria for the output?
<--- Score

42. Is there an established change management process?
<--- Score

43. What are your Risks Dashboard processes?
<--- Score

44. What, related to, Risks Dashboard processes does your organization outsource?
<--- Score

45. What is the oversight process?
<--- Score

46. Should you invest in industry-recognized qualifications?
<--- Score

47. What successful thing are you doing today that may be blinding you to new growth opportunities?
<--- Score

48. What is your organizations process which leads to recognition of value generation?
<--- Score

49. What are the disruptive Risks Dashboard technologies that enable your organization to radically change your business processes?
<--- Score

50. How do mission and objectives affect the Risks Dashboard processes of your organization?
<--- Score

51. What will drive Risks Dashboard change?
<--- Score

52. What systems/processes must you excel at?
<--- Score

53. How do you ensure that the Risks Dashboard opportunity is realistic?
<--- Score

54. What are the Risks Dashboard business drivers?
<--- Score

55. How do you implement and manage your work processes to ensure that they meet design requirements?
<--- Score

56. Were Pareto charts (or similar) used to portray the 'heavy hitters' (or key sources of variation)?
<--- Score

57. What quality tools were used to get through the analyze phase?
<--- Score

58. What qualifications are needed?
<--- Score

59. What is the output?
<--- Score

60. Who owns what data?
<--- Score

61. Which Risks Dashboard data should be retained?
<--- Score

62. Where is Risks Dashboard data gathered?
<--- Score

63. Do your employees have the opportunity to do what they do best everyday?
<--- Score

64. Is the Risks Dashboard process severely broken such that a re-design is necessary?
<--- Score

65. What are your current levels and trends in key Risks Dashboard measures or indicators of product and process performance that are important to and directly serve your customers?
<--- Score

66. Is the gap/opportunity displayed and communicated in financial terms?
<--- Score

67. What process should you select for improvement?
<--- Score

68. What are the necessary qualifications?
<--- Score

69. What Risks Dashboard data will be collected?
<--- Score

70. Identify an operational issue in your organization, for example, could a particular task be done more quickly or more efficiently by Risks Dashboard?
<--- Score

71. Who will gather what data?
<--- Score

72. What Risks Dashboard metrics are outputs of the process?
<--- Score

73. Is there any way to speed up the process?
<--- Score

74. What does the data say about the performance of the stakeholder process?
<--- Score

75. How is the data gathered?
<--- Score

76. What were the financial benefits resulting from any 'ground fruit or low-hanging fruit' (quick fixes)?
<--- Score

77. What Risks Dashboard data do you gather or use now?
<--- Score

78. How do you identify specific Risks Dashboard investment opportunities and emerging trends?
<--- Score

79. An organizationally feasible system request is one that considers the mission, goals and objectives of the organization, key questions are: is the Risks Dashboard solution request practical and will it solve a problem or take advantage of an opportunity to achieve company goals?
<--- Score

80. Where can you get qualified talent today?
<--- Score

81. Do you, as a leader, bounce back quickly from setbacks?
<--- Score

82. Do you have the authority to produce the output?
<--- Score

83. Do your leaders quickly bounce back from setbacks?
<--- Score

84. Do quality systems drive continuous improvement?
<--- Score

85. How does the organization define, manage, and improve its Risks Dashboard processes?
<--- Score

86. Do your contracts/agreements contain data

security obligations?
<--- Score

87. How is the Risks Dashboard Value Stream Mapping managed?
<--- Score

88. How will the Risks Dashboard data be captured?
<--- Score

89. What output to create?
<--- Score

90. Was a cause-and-effect diagram used to explore the different types of causes (or sources of variation)?
<--- Score

91. What tools were used to generate the list of possible causes?
<--- Score

92. Do you understand your management processes today?
<--- Score

93. What other jobs or tasks affect the performance of the steps in the Risks Dashboard process?
<--- Score

94. What qualifies as competition?
<--- Score

95. What are the best opportunities for value improvement?
<--- Score

96. What is the cost of poor quality as supported by the team's analysis?

<--- Score

97. Who is involved in the management review process?

<--- Score

98. Are all team members qualified for all tasks?

<--- Score

99. How do you measure the operational performance of your key work systems and processes, including productivity, cycle time, and other appropriate measures of process effectiveness, efficiency, and innovation?

<--- Score

100. Is the required Risks Dashboard data gathered?

<--- Score

101. What did the team gain from developing a sub-process map?

<--- Score

102. Is data and process analysis, root cause analysis and quantifying the gap/opportunity in place?

<--- Score

103. Do several people in different organizational units assist with the Risks Dashboard process?

<--- Score

104. How do your work systems and key work processes relate to and capitalize on your core competencies?

<--- Score

105. What are the revised rough estimates of the financial savings/opportunity for Risks Dashboard improvements?
<--- Score

106. Were any designed experiments used to generate additional insight into the data analysis?
<--- Score

107. How is the way you as the leader think and process information affecting your organizational culture?
<--- Score

108. What are the personnel training and qualifications required?
<--- Score

109. Think about the functions involved in your Risks Dashboard project, what processes flow from these functions?
<--- Score

110. Is the suppliers process defined and controlled?
<--- Score

111. Is there a strict change management process?
<--- Score

112. What is the Value Stream Mapping?
<--- Score

113. What is the Risks Dashboard Driver?

<--- Score

114. What controls do you have in place to protect data?
<--- Score

115. What are your outputs?
<--- Score

116. Is the final output clearly identified?
<--- Score

117. Has an output goal been set?
<--- Score

118. How can risk management be tied procedurally to process elements?
<--- Score

119. How are outputs preserved and protected?
<--- Score

120. Have you defined which data is gathered how?
<--- Score

121. What is the complexity of the output produced?
<--- Score

122. Are all staff in core Risks Dashboard subjects Highly Qualified?
<--- Score

123. What tools were used to narrow the list of possible causes?
<--- Score

124. Who is involved with workflow mapping?
<--- Score

125. Is pre-qualification of suppliers carried out?
<--- Score

126. What methods do you use to gather Risks Dashboard data?
<--- Score

127. What resources go in to get the desired output?
<--- Score

128. How is Risks Dashboard data gathered?
<--- Score

129. Has data output been validated?
<--- Score

130. What are your best practices for minimizing Risks Dashboard project risk, while demonstrating incremental value and quick wins throughout the Risks Dashboard project lifecycle?
<--- Score

Add up total points for this section:
_ _ _ _ _ = Total points for this section

Divided by: _ _ _ _ _ _ (number of statements answered) = _ _ _ _ _ _
Average score for this section

Transfer your score to the Risks Dashboard Index at the beginning of the Self-Assessment.

CRITERION #5: IMPROVE:

In my belief, the answer to this question is clearly defined:

5 Strongly Agree

4 Agree

3 Neutral

2 Disagree

1 Strongly Disagree

1. Which of the recognised risks out of all risks can be most likely transferred?
<--- Score

2. Who do you report Risks Dashboard results to?
<--- Score

3. What can you do to improve?
<--- Score

4. What practices helps your organization to develop its capacity to recognize patterns?
<--- Score

5. What is the team's contingency plan for potential problems occurring in implementation?
<--- Score

6. What error proofing will be done to address some of the discrepancies observed in the 'as is' process?
<--- Score

7. Who makes the Risks Dashboard decisions in your organization?
<--- Score

8. Who are the people involved in developing and implementing Risks Dashboard?
<--- Score

9. Would you develop a Risks Dashboard Communication Strategy?
<--- Score

10. Risks Dashboard risk decisions: whose call Is It?
<--- Score

11. Risk events: what are the things that could go wrong?
<--- Score

12. What strategies for Risks Dashboard improvement are successful?
<--- Score

13. What should a proof of concept or pilot accomplish?
<--- Score

14. What current systems have to be understood and/ or changed?
<--- Score

15. How do you mitigate Risks Dashboard risk?
<--- Score

16. How will you know that you have improved?
<--- Score

17. What is the risk?
<--- Score

18. Where do the Risks Dashboard decisions reside?
<--- Score

19. Can you identify any significant risks or exposures to Risks Dashboard third- parties (vendors, service providers, alliance partners etc) that concern you?
<--- Score

20. How do you keep improving Risks Dashboard?
<--- Score

21. Is Risks Dashboard documentation maintained?
<--- Score

22. How do you deal with Risks Dashboard risk?
<--- Score

23. Is there any other Risks Dashboard solution?

<--- Score

24. Who manages Risks Dashboard risk?
<--- Score

25. What were the underlying assumptions on the cost-benefit analysis?
<--- Score

26. What were the criteria for evaluating a Risks Dashboard pilot?
<--- Score

27. What does the 'should be' process map/design look like?
<--- Score

28. In the past few months, what is the smallest change you have made that has had the biggest positive result? What was it about that small change that produced the large return?
<--- Score

29. Was a pilot designed for the proposed solution(s)?
<--- Score

30. At what point will vulnerability assessments be performed once Risks Dashboard is put into production (e.g., ongoing Risk Management after implementation)?
<--- Score

31. How do you manage Risks Dashboard risk?
<--- Score

32. What are the implications of the one critical Risks

Dashboard decision 10 minutes, 10 months, and 10 years from now?

<--- Score

33. Is a solution implementation plan established, including schedule/work breakdown structure, resources, risk management plan, cost/budget, and control plan?

<--- Score

34. Are you assessing Risks Dashboard and risk?

<--- Score

35. What do you want to improve?

<--- Score

36. Can you integrate quality management and risk management?

<--- Score

37. Who are the key stakeholders for the Risks Dashboard evaluation?

<--- Score

38. Is supporting Risks Dashboard documentation required?

<--- Score

39. What improvements have been achieved?

<--- Score

40. How do you manage and improve your Risks Dashboard work systems to deliver customer value and achieve organizational success and sustainability?

<--- Score

41. When you map the key players in your own work and the types/domains of relationships with them, which relationships do you find easy and which challenging, and why?
<--- Score

42. Is risk periodically assessed?
<--- Score

43. How risky is your organization?
<--- Score

44. Are procedures documented for managing Risks Dashboard risks?
<--- Score

45. What is the magnitude of the improvements?
<--- Score

46. Is the implementation plan designed?
<--- Score

47. What tools were most useful during the improve phase?
<--- Score

48. What Risks Dashboard improvements can be made?
<--- Score

49. Who are the Risks Dashboard decision makers?
<--- Score

50. Explorations of the frontiers of Risks Dashboard will help you build influence, improve Risks

Dashboard, optimize decision making, and sustain change, what is your approach?
<--- Score

51. What are the concrete Risks Dashboard results?
<--- Score

52. Who controls key decisions that will be made?
<--- Score

53. Do you need to do a usability evaluation?
<--- Score

54. How can the phases of Risks Dashboard development be identified?
<--- Score

55. How will you measure the results?
<--- Score

56. What are the Risks Dashboard security risks?
<--- Score

57. What resources are required for the improvement efforts?
<--- Score

58. Who controls the risk?
<--- Score

59. Are risk triggers captured?
<--- Score

60. How are policy decisions made and where?
<--- Score

61. Are events managed to resolution?
<--- Score

62. How do you define the solutions' scope?
<--- Score

63. How are Risks Dashboard risks managed?
<--- Score

64. Have you achieved Risks Dashboard improvements?
<--- Score

65. Is there a small-scale pilot for proposed improvement(s)? What conclusions were drawn from the outcomes of a pilot?
<--- Score

66. What are your current levels and trends in key measures or indicators of workforce and leader development?
<--- Score

67. Is pilot data collected and analyzed?
<--- Score

68. Were any criteria developed to assist the team in testing and evaluating potential solutions?
<--- Score

69. Will the controls trigger any other risks?
<--- Score

70. What is the Risks Dashboard's sustainability risk?
<--- Score

71. Have you identified breakpoints and/or risk tolerances that will trigger broad consideration of a potential need for intervention or modification of strategy?
<--- Score

72. Is the scope clearly documented?
<--- Score

73. What area needs the greatest improvement?
<--- Score

74. What is Risks Dashboard's impact on utilizing the best solution(s)?
<--- Score

75. How is continuous improvement applied to risk management?
<--- Score

76. Does a good decision guarantee a good outcome?
<--- Score

77. How do you measure improved Risks Dashboard service perception, and satisfaction?
<--- Score

78. How do the Risks Dashboard results compare with the performance of your competitors and other organizations with similar offerings?
<--- Score

79. Who will be responsible for documenting the Risks Dashboard requirements in detail?

<--- Score

80. How do you improve productivity?
<--- Score

81. How do you measure risk?
<--- Score

82. How will you recognize and celebrate results?
<--- Score

83. Where do you need Risks Dashboard improvement?
<--- Score

84. To what extent does management recognize Risks Dashboard as a tool to increase the results?
<--- Score

85. If you could go back in time five years, what decision would you make differently? What is your best guess as to what decision you're making today you might regret five years from now?
<--- Score

86. What tools were used to evaluate the potential solutions?
<--- Score

87. How will you know when its improved?
<--- Score

88. Who should make the Risks Dashboard decisions?
<--- Score

89. Are the risks fully understood, reasonable and

manageable?
<--- Score

90. Is the Risks Dashboard solution sustainable?
<--- Score

91. How can you improve Risks Dashboard?
<--- Score

92. Is the solution technically practical?
<--- Score

93. What assumptions are made about the solution and approach?
<--- Score

94. What went well, what should change, what can improve?
<--- Score

95. Risk Identification: What are the possible risk events your organization faces in relation to Risks Dashboard?
<--- Score

96. Risk factors: what are the characteristics of Risks Dashboard that make it risky?
<--- Score

97. Was a Risks Dashboard charter developed?
<--- Score

98. Is the optimal solution selected based on testing and analysis?
<--- Score

99. How do you improve your likelihood of success ?
<--- Score

100. What tools were used to tap into the creativity and encourage 'outside the box' thinking?
<--- Score

101. What risks do you need to manage?
<--- Score

102. For decision problems, how do you develop a decision statement?
<--- Score

103. Who manages supplier risk management in your organization?
<--- Score

104. How do you go about comparing Risks Dashboard approaches/solutions?
<--- Score

105. Who are the Risks Dashboard decision-makers?
<--- Score

106. Is any Risks Dashboard documentation required?
<--- Score

107. How can you improve performance?
<--- Score

108. How significant is the improvement in the eyes of the end user?
<--- Score

109. What actually has to improve and by how much?
<--- Score

110. How do you improve Risks Dashboard service perception, and satisfaction?
<--- Score

111. Which Risks Dashboard solution is appropriate?
<--- Score

112. Do vendor agreements bring new compliance risk ?
<--- Score

113. How can you better manage risk?
<--- Score

114. Do you cover the five essential competencies: Communication, Collaboration,Innovation, Adaptability, and Leadership that improve an organizations ability to leverage the new Risks Dashboard in a volatile global economy?
<--- Score

115. Is there a cost/benefit analysis of optimal solution(s)?
<--- Score

116. What is Risks Dashboard risk?
<--- Score

117. What communications are necessary to support the implementation of the solution?
<--- Score

118. What to do with the results or outcomes of measurements?
<--- Score

119. What criteria will you use to assess your Risks Dashboard risks?
<--- Score

120. How can skill-level changes improve Risks Dashboard?
<--- Score

121. What attendant changes will need to be made to ensure that the solution is successful?
<--- Score

122. Do those selected for the Risks Dashboard team have a good general understanding of what Risks Dashboard is all about?
<--- Score

123. Is the measure of success for Risks Dashboard understandable to a variety of people?
<--- Score

124. Is a contingency plan established?
<--- Score

125. How do you measure progress and evaluate training effectiveness?
<--- Score

126. How will you know that a change is an improvement?
<--- Score

127. Why improve in the first place?
<--- Score

128. What needs improvement? Why?
<--- Score

129. What lessons, if any, from a pilot were incorporated into the design of the full-scale solution?
<--- Score

130. How does your organization evaluate strategic Risks Dashboard success?
<--- Score

131. Is there a high likelihood that any recommendations will achieve their intended results?
<--- Score

132. Is the Risks Dashboard risk managed?
<--- Score

133. Does the goal represent a desired result that can be measured?
<--- Score

134. Is the Risks Dashboard documentation thorough?
<--- Score

135. Who will be using the results of the measurement activities?
<--- Score

136. For estimation problems, how do you develop an estimation statement?
<--- Score

137. Who will be responsible for making the decisions to include or exclude requested changes once Risks Dashboard is underway?
<--- Score

138. What is the implementation plan?
<--- Score

139. How do you link measurement and risk?
<--- Score

Add up total points for this section:
_ _ _ _ _ = Total points for this section

Divided by: _ _ _ _ _ _ (number of statements answered) = _ _ _ _ _ _
Average score for this section

Transfer your score to the Risks Dashboard Index at the beginning of the Self-Assessment.

CRITERION #6: CONTROL:

INTENT: Implement the practical solution. Maintain the performance and correct possible complications.

In my belief, the answer to this question is clearly defined:

5 Strongly Agree

4 Agree

3 Neutral

2 Disagree

1 Strongly Disagree

1. Are new process steps, standards, and documentation ingrained into normal operations?
<--- Score

2. What is the best design framework for Risks Dashboard organization now that, in a post industrial-age if the top-down, command and control model is no longer relevant?
<--- Score

3. Are you measuring, monitoring and predicting Risks Dashboard activities to optimize operations and profitability, and enhancing outcomes?
<--- Score

4. What Risks Dashboard standards are applicable?
<--- Score

5. What are customers monitoring?
<--- Score

6. How do controls support value?
<--- Score

7. Are operating procedures consistent?
<--- Score

8. Are there documented procedures?
<--- Score

9. Are the Risks Dashboard standards challenging?
<--- Score

10. How do senior leaders actions reflect a commitment to the organizations Risks Dashboard values?
<--- Score

11. How will the process owner verify improvement in present and future sigma levels, process capabilities?
<--- Score

12. Is there a recommended audit plan for routine surveillance inspections of Risks Dashboard's gains?
<--- Score

13. Is reporting being used or needed?
<--- Score

14. Can support from partners be adjusted?
<--- Score

15. How do you monitor usage and cost?
<--- Score

16. How do your controls stack up?
<--- Score

17. Do the Risks Dashboard decisions you make today help people and the planet tomorrow?
<--- Score

18. What is the control/monitoring plan?
<--- Score

19. Is there documentation that will support the successful operation of the improvement?
<--- Score

20. Is there a Risks Dashboard Communication plan covering who needs to get what information when?
<--- Score

21. What other systems, operations, processes, and infrastructures (hiring practices, staffing, training, incentives/rewards, metrics/dashboards/scorecards, etc.) need updates, additions, changes, or deletions in order to facilitate knowledge transfer and improvements?
<--- Score

22. What other areas of the group might benefit from the Risks Dashboard team's improvements, knowledge, and learning?
<--- Score

23. How will the day-to-day responsibilities for monitoring and continual improvement be transferred from the improvement team to the process owner?
<--- Score

24. What key inputs and outputs are being measured on an ongoing basis?
<--- Score

25. What are the known security controls?
<--- Score

26. What is the standard for acceptable Risks Dashboard performance?
<--- Score

27. Are the planned controls in place?
<--- Score

28. How might the group capture best practices and lessons learned so as to leverage improvements?
<--- Score

29. What is your theory of human motivation, and how does your compensation plan fit with that view?
<--- Score

30. Does Risks Dashboard appropriately measure and monitor risk?
<--- Score

31. How do you select, collect, align, and integrate Risks Dashboard data and information for tracking daily operations and overall organizational performance, including progress relative to strategic objectives and action plans?
<--- Score

32. Does the response plan contain a definite closed loop continual improvement scheme (e.g., plan-do-check-act)?
<--- Score

33. What is your plan to assess your security risks?
<--- Score

34. What is the recommended frequency of auditing?
<--- Score

35. Is there a control plan in place for sustaining improvements (short and long-term)?
<--- Score

36. Is there a standardized process?
<--- Score

37. Implementation Planning: is a pilot needed to test the changes before a full roll out occurs?
<--- Score

38. Have new or revised work instructions resulted?
<--- Score

39. Is there a documented and implemented monitoring plan?
<--- Score

40. Who is the Risks Dashboard process owner?
<--- Score

41. You may have created your quality measures at a time when you lacked resources, technology wasn't up to the required standard, or low service levels were the industry norm. Have those circumstances changed?
<--- Score

42. Do you monitor the Risks Dashboard decisions made and fine tune them as they evolve?
<--- Score

43. How can you best use all of your knowledge repositories to enhance learning and sharing?
<--- Score

44. Will any special training be provided for results interpretation?
<--- Score

45. Is there a transfer of ownership and knowledge to process owner and process team tasked with the responsibilities.
<--- Score

46. What should the next improvement project be that is related to Risks Dashboard?
<--- Score

47. Does job training on the documented procedures need to be part of the process team's education and training?
<--- Score

48. Are the planned controls working?

<--- Score

49. How will Risks Dashboard decisions be made and monitored?

<--- Score

50. How do you encourage people to take control and responsibility?

<--- Score

51. How likely is the current Risks Dashboard plan to come in on schedule or on budget?

<--- Score

52. What do you stand for--and what are you against?

<--- Score

53. What are your results for key measures or indicators of the accomplishment of your Risks Dashboard strategy and action plans, including building and strengthening core competencies?

<--- Score

54. How is change control managed?

<--- Score

55. Will the team be available to assist members in planning investigations?

<--- Score

56. Who will be in control?

<--- Score

57. In the case of a Risks Dashboard project, the criteria for the audit derive from implementation objectives, an audit of a Risks Dashboard project involves assessing whether the recommendations outlined for implementation have been met, can you track that any Risks Dashboard project is implemented as planned, and is it working?
<--- Score

58. Against what alternative is success being measured?
<--- Score

59. What do your reports reflect?
<--- Score

60. How will report readings be checked to effectively monitor performance?
<--- Score

61. What are the key elements of your Risks Dashboard performance improvement system, including your evaluation, organizational learning, and innovation processes?
<--- Score

62. Does the Risks Dashboard performance meet the customer's requirements?
<--- Score

63. How do you establish and deploy modified action plans if circumstances require a shift in plans and rapid execution of new plans?
<--- Score

64. How will the process owner and team be able to

hold the gains?
<--- Score

65. Are documented procedures clear and easy to follow for the operators?
<--- Score

66. Who sets the Risks Dashboard standards?
<--- Score

67. What adjustments to the strategies are needed?
<--- Score

68. Is new knowledge gained imbedded in the response plan?
<--- Score

69. Is there an action plan in case of emergencies?
<--- Score

70. Can you adapt and adjust to changing Risks Dashboard situations?
<--- Score

71. Are controls in place and consistently applied?
<--- Score

72. Who controls critical resources?
<--- Score

73. Does a troubleshooting guide exist or is it needed?
<--- Score

74. What do you measure to verify effectiveness gains?
<--- Score

75. Will existing staff require re-training, for example, to learn new business processes?
<--- Score

76. How do you plan for the cost of succession?
<--- Score

77. Where do ideas that reach policy makers and planners as proposals for Risks Dashboard strengthening and reform actually originate?
<--- Score

78. What are you attempting to measure/monitor?
<--- Score

79. Will your goals reflect your program budget?
<--- Score

80. Are pertinent alerts monitored, analyzed and distributed to appropriate personnel?
<--- Score

81. Do you monitor the effectiveness of your Risks Dashboard activities?
<--- Score

82. Has the improved process and its steps been standardized?
<--- Score

83. What are the critical parameters to watch?
<--- Score

84. How is Risks Dashboard project cost planned, managed, monitored?

<--- Score

85. How will new or emerging customer needs/ requirements be checked/communicated to orient the process toward meeting the new specifications and continually reducing variation?
<--- Score

86. How will input, process, and output variables be checked to detect for sub-optimal conditions?
<--- Score

87. How will you measure your QA plan's effectiveness?
<--- Score

88. Is a response plan in place for when the input, process, or output measures indicate an 'out-of-control' condition?
<--- Score

89. What quality tools were useful in the control phase?
<--- Score

90. Are suggested corrective/restorative actions indicated on the response plan for known causes to problems that might surface?
<--- Score

91. Is a response plan established and deployed?
<--- Score

92. What should you measure to verify efficiency gains?
<--- Score

93. Has the Risks Dashboard value of standards been quantified?
<--- Score

94. What can you control?
<--- Score

95. Is the Risks Dashboard test/monitoring cost justified?
<--- Score

96. Is knowledge gained on process shared and institutionalized?
<--- Score

97. Act/Adjust: What Do you Need to Do Differently?
<--- Score

98. Who has control over resources?
<--- Score

Add up total points for this section:
_ _ _ _ _ = Total points for this section

Divided by: _ _ _ _ _ _ (number of statements answered) = _ _ _ _ _ _
Average score for this section

Transfer your score to the Risks Dashboard Index at the beginning of the Self-Assessment.

CRITERION #7: SUSTAIN:

INTENT: Retain the benefits.

In my belief, the answer to this question is clearly defined:

5 Strongly Agree

4 Agree

3 Neutral

2 Disagree

1 Strongly Disagree

1. What are the success criteria that will indicate that Risks Dashboard objectives have been met and the benefits delivered?
<--- Score

2. Who will determine interim and final deadlines?
<--- Score

3. How do senior leaders deploy your organizations vision and values through your leadership system, to the workforce, to key suppliers and partners, and to

customers and other stakeholders, as appropriate?
<--- Score

4. Do you say no to customers for no reason?
<--- Score

5. What is an unauthorized commitment?
<--- Score

6. What are your most important goals for the strategic Risks Dashboard objectives?
<--- Score

7. Can you break it down?
<--- Score

8. What is your competitive advantage?
<--- Score

9. How do you deal with Risks Dashboard changes?
<--- Score

10. If you got fired and a new hire took your place, what would she do different?
<--- Score

11. Is it economical; do you have the time and money?
<--- Score

12. How do you transition from the baseline to the target?
<--- Score

13. What is the kind of project structure that would be appropriate for your Risks Dashboard project,

should it be formal and complex, or can it be less formal and relatively simple?
<--- Score

14. Why will customers want to buy your organizations products/services?
<--- Score

15. How do you manage Risks Dashboard Knowledge Management (KM)?
<--- Score

16. Whom among your colleagues do you trust, and for what?
<--- Score

17. Is there a work around that you can use?
<--- Score

18. What stupid rule would you most like to kill?
<--- Score

19. What threat is Risks Dashboard addressing?
<--- Score

20. Do you have the right people on the bus?
<--- Score

21. Who are the key stakeholders?
<--- Score

22. Would you rather sell to knowledgeable and informed customers or to uninformed customers?
<--- Score

23. Who is going to spread your message?

<--- Score

24. What have you done to protect your business from competitive encroachment?
<--- Score

25. Who, on the executive team or the board, has spoken to a customer recently?
<--- Score

26. Who is responsible for ensuring appropriate resources (time, people and money) are allocated to Risks Dashboard?
<--- Score

27. Political -is anyone trying to undermine this project?
<--- Score

28. What knowledge, skills and characteristics mark a good Risks Dashboard project manager?
<--- Score

29. What are the barriers to increased Risks Dashboard production?
<--- Score

30. Who have you, as a company, historically been when you've been at your best?
<--- Score

31. What would you recommend your friend do if he/she were facing this dilemma?
<--- Score

32. Are the criteria for selecting recommendations

stated?

<--- Score

33. Ask yourself: how would you do this work if you only had one staff member to do it?

<--- Score

34. How can you become the company that would put you out of business?

<--- Score

35. Who do you think the world wants your organization to be?

<--- Score

36. Is maximizing Risks Dashboard protection the same as minimizing Risks Dashboard loss?

<--- Score

37. Who uses your product in ways you never expected?

<--- Score

38. What are specific Risks Dashboard rules to follow?

<--- Score

39. If you were responsible for initiating and implementing major changes in your organization, what steps might you take to ensure acceptance of those changes?

<--- Score

40. How do you accomplish your long range Risks Dashboard goals?

<--- Score

41. How will you insure seamless interoperability of Risks Dashboard moving forward?
<--- Score

42. What is the range of capabilities?
<--- Score

43. Do you see more potential in people than they do in themselves?
<--- Score

44. What may be the consequences for the performance of an organization if all stakeholders are not consulted regarding Risks Dashboard?
<--- Score

45. How can you incorporate support to ensure safe and effective use of Risks Dashboard into the services that you provide?
<--- Score

46. What would have to be true for the option on the table to be the best possible choice?
<--- Score

47. How is implementation research currently incorporated into each of your goals?
<--- Score

48. What is effective Risks Dashboard?
<--- Score

49. What are strategies for increasing support and reducing opposition?
<--- Score

50. How can you negotiate Risks Dashboard successfully with a stubborn boss, an irate client, or a deceitful coworker?

<--- Score

51. Is Risks Dashboard dependent on the successful delivery of a current project?

<--- Score

52. What is a feasible sequencing of reform initiatives over time?

<--- Score

53. What business benefits will Risks Dashboard goals deliver if achieved?

<--- Score

54. How do you create buy-in?

<--- Score

55. What are the key enablers to make this Risks Dashboard move?

<--- Score

56. What is the purpose of Risks Dashboard in relation to the mission?

<--- Score

57. What is the overall business strategy?

<--- Score

58. How will you motivate the stakeholders with the least vested interest?

<--- Score

59. How do you decide how much to remunerate an

employee?
<--- Score

60. What goals did you miss?
<--- Score

61. What are your personal philosophies regarding Risks Dashboard and how do they influence your work?
<--- Score

62. Will it be accepted by users?
<--- Score

63. Do you have past Risks Dashboard successes?
<--- Score

64. Who do we want your customers to become?
<--- Score

65. How likely is it that a customer would recommend your company to a friend or colleague?
<--- Score

66. Which functions and people interact with the supplier and or customer?
<--- Score

67. Are your responses positive or negative?
<--- Score

68. What are current Risks Dashboard paradigms?
<--- Score

69. Are assumptions made in Risks Dashboard stated explicitly?

<--- Score

70. Will there be any necessary staff changes (redundancies or new hires)?
<--- Score

71. What was the last experiment you ran?
<--- Score

72. What will be the consequences to the stakeholder (financial, reputation etc) if Risks Dashboard does not go ahead or fails to deliver the objectives?
<--- Score

73. Why should people listen to you?
<--- Score

74. What are the short and long-term Risks Dashboard goals?
<--- Score

75. How do you track customer value, profitability or financial return, organizational success, and sustainability?
<--- Score

76. How do you know if you are successful?
<--- Score

77. Who will provide the final approval of Risks Dashboard deliverables?
<--- Score

78. What is the source of the strategies for Risks Dashboard strengthening and reform?
<--- Score

79. What potential megatrends could make your business model obsolete?

<--- Score

80. If there were zero limitations, what would you do differently?

<--- Score

81. How much contingency will be available in the budget?

<--- Score

82. What Risks Dashboard skills are most important?

<--- Score

83. If your customer were your grandmother, would you tell her to buy what you're selling?

<--- Score

84. How do you keep the momentum going?

<--- Score

85. Are you relevant? Will you be relevant five years from now? Ten?

<--- Score

86. How do you ensure that implementations of Risks Dashboard products are done in a way that ensures safety?

<--- Score

87. If you do not follow, then how to lead?

<--- Score

88. How are you doing compared to your industry?

<--- Score

89. How do you cross-sell and up-sell your Risks Dashboard success?
<--- Score

90. How long will it take to change?
<--- Score

91. Who are your customers?
<--- Score

92. What is it like to work for you?
<--- Score

93. Operational - will it work?
<--- Score

94. Can the schedule be done in the given time?
<--- Score

95. What are the essentials of internal Risks Dashboard management?
<--- Score

96. What projects are going on in the organization today, and what resources are those projects using from the resource pools?
<--- Score

97. Marketing budgets are tighter, consumers are more skeptical, and social media has changed forever the way we talk about Risks Dashboard, how do you gain traction?
<--- Score

98. How do you govern and fulfill your societal responsibilities?
<--- Score

99. What are the performance and scale of the Risks Dashboard tools?
<--- Score

100. Do you have the right capabilities and capacities?
<--- Score

101. What is your Risks Dashboard strategy?
<--- Score

102. What are you challenging?
<--- Score

103. Why not do Risks Dashboard?
<--- Score

104. Are the assumptions believable and achievable?
<--- Score

105. What Risks Dashboard modifications can you make work for you?
<--- Score

106. Is Risks Dashboard realistic, or are you setting yourself up for failure?
<--- Score

107. What is your BATNA (best alternative to a negotiated agreement)?
<--- Score

108. Who is the main stakeholder, with ultimate responsibility for driving Risks Dashboard forward?

<--- Score

109. How do you foster the skills, knowledge, talents, attributes, and characteristics you want to have?

<--- Score

110. In retrospect, of the projects that you pulled the plug on, what percent do you wish had been allowed to keep going, and what percent do you wish had ended earlier?

<--- Score

111. What happens at your organization when people fail?

<--- Score

112. Instead of going to current contacts for new ideas, what if you reconnected with dormant contacts--the people you used to know? If you were going reactivate a dormant tie, who would it be?

<--- Score

113. Are you making progress, and are you making progress as Risks Dashboard leaders?

<--- Score

114. Why do and why don't your customers like your organization?

<--- Score

115. Who else should you help?

<--- Score

116. How do you provide a safe environment -physically and emotionally?
<--- Score

117. Who will be responsible for deciding whether Risks Dashboard goes ahead or not after the initial investigations?
<--- Score

118. Why is Risks Dashboard important for you now?
<--- Score

119. What are internal and external Risks Dashboard relations?
<--- Score

120. In a project to restructure Risks Dashboard outcomes, which stakeholders would you involve?
<--- Score

121. Do you have enough freaky customers in your portfolio pushing you to the limit day in and day out?
<--- Score

122. What are you trying to prove to yourself, and how might it be hijacking your life and business success?
<--- Score

123. Where can you break convention?
<--- Score

124. Do you think Risks Dashboard accomplishes the goals you expect it to accomplish?

<--- Score

125. How important is Risks Dashboard to the user organizations mission?
<--- Score

126. Is the Risks Dashboard organization completing tasks effectively and efficiently?
<--- Score

127. Who is responsible for Risks Dashboard?
<--- Score

128. What is the craziest thing you can do?
<--- Score

129. How do customers see your organization?
<--- Score

130. When information truly is ubiquitous, when reach and connectivity are completely global, when computing resources are infinite, and when a whole new set of impossibilities are not only possible, but happening, what will that do to your business?
<--- Score

131. How do you make it meaningful in connecting Risks Dashboard with what users do day-to-day?
<--- Score

132. How do you proactively clarify deliverables and Risks Dashboard quality expectations?
<--- Score

133. What you are going to do to affect the numbers?

<--- Score

134. Can you do all this work?
<--- Score

135. What is the overall talent health of your organization as a whole at senior levels, and for each organization reporting to a member of the Senior Leadership Team?
<--- Score

136. How do you maintain Risks Dashboard's Integrity?
<--- Score

137. What are the rules and assumptions your industry operates under? What if the opposite were true?
<--- Score

138. What is the funding source for this project?
<--- Score

139. What counts that you are not counting?
<--- Score

140. What one word do you want to own in the minds of your customers, employees, and partners?
<--- Score

141. How do you keep records, of what?
<--- Score

142. How can you become more high-tech but still be high touch?
<--- Score

143. What is your formula for success in Risks Dashboard ?

<--- Score

144. If you weren't already in this business, would you enter it today? And if not, what are you going to do about it?

<--- Score

145. Who is on the team?

<--- Score

146. What are the gaps in your knowledge and experience?

<--- Score

147. What are the challenges?

<--- Score

148. Can you maintain your growth without detracting from the factors that have contributed to your success?

<--- Score

149. What are the top 3 things at the forefront of your Risks Dashboard agendas for the next 3 years?

<--- Score

150. Which individuals, teams or departments will be involved in Risks Dashboard?

<--- Score

151. What have been your experiences in defining long range Risks Dashboard goals?

<--- Score

152. Who are four people whose careers you have enhanced?
<--- Score

153. Think of your Risks Dashboard project, what are the main functions?
<--- Score

154. How will you know that the Risks Dashboard project has been successful?
<--- Score

155. Do you feel that more should be done in the Risks Dashboard area?
<--- Score

156. How do you lead with Risks Dashboard in mind?
<--- Score

157. What does your signature ensure?
<--- Score

158. Are all key stakeholders present at all Structured Walkthroughs?
<--- Score

159. Who do you want your customers to become?
<--- Score

160. How do you determine the key elements that affect Risks Dashboard workforce satisfaction, how are these elements determined for different workforce groups and segments?
<--- Score

161. What happens if you do not have enough funding?

<--- Score

162. Whose voice (department, ethnic group, women, older workers, etc) might you have missed hearing from in your company, and how might you amplify this voice to create positive momentum for your business?

<--- Score

163. What information is critical to your organization that your executives are ignoring?

<--- Score

164. Why is it important to have senior management support for a Risks Dashboard project?

<--- Score

165. What must you excel at?

<--- Score

166. Is your basic point _____ or _____?

<--- Score

167. Are you satisfied with your current role? If not, what is missing from it?

<--- Score

168. How do you set Risks Dashboard stretch targets and how do you get people to not only participate in setting these stretch targets but also that they strive to achieve these?

<--- Score

169. How do you engage the workforce, in addition to satisfying them?

<--- Score

170. Is there any reason to believe the opposite of my current belief?

<--- Score

171. What is the estimated value of the project?

<--- Score

172. What is your question? Why?

<--- Score

173. Is a Risks Dashboard team work effort in place?

<--- Score

174. Are you using a design thinking approach and integrating Innovation, Risks Dashboard Experience, and Brand Value?

<--- Score

175. What are the long-term Risks Dashboard goals?

<--- Score

176. What are the potential basics of Risks Dashboard fraud?

<--- Score

177. What happens when a new employee joins the organization?

<--- Score

178. What new services of functionality will be implemented next with Risks Dashboard ?

<--- Score

179. What should you stop doing?
<--- Score

180. Are you / should you be revolutionary or evolutionary?
<--- Score

181. At what moment would you think; Will I get fired?
<--- Score

182. How do you go about securing Risks Dashboard?
<--- Score

183. Which models, tools and techniques are necessary?
<--- Score

184. What did you miss in the interview for the worst hire you ever made?
<--- Score

185. To whom do you add value?
<--- Score

186. How will you ensure you get what you expected?
<--- Score

187. If you had to leave your organization for a year and the only communication you could have with employees/colleagues was a single paragraph, what would you write?
<--- Score

188. What could happen if you do not do it?
<--- Score

189. How do you foster innovation?

<--- Score

190. If no one would ever find out about your accomplishments, how would you lead differently?

<--- Score

191. If you find that you havent accomplished one of the goals for one of the steps of the Risks Dashboard strategy, what will you do to fix it?

<--- Score

192. What management system can you use to leverage the Risks Dashboard experience, ideas, and concerns of the people closest to the work to be done?

<--- Score

193. What unique value proposition (UVP) do you offer?

<--- Score

194. Is your strategy driving your strategy? Or is the way in which you allocate resources driving your strategy?

<--- Score

Add up total points for this section:
_ _ _ _ _ = Total points for this section

Divided by: _ _ _ _ _ _ (number of statements answered) = _ _ _ _ _ _
Average score for this section

Transfer your score to the Risks

Dashboard Index at the beginning of the
Self-Assessment.

Risks Dashboard and Managing Projects, Criteria for Project Managers:

1.0 Initiating Process Group: Risks Dashboard

1. The process to Manage Stakeholders is part of which process group?

2. Have the stakeholders identified all individual requirements pertaining to business process?

3. Have requirements been tested, approved, and fulfill the Risks Dashboard project scope?

4. Who supports, improves, and oversees standardized processes related to the Risks Dashboard projects program?

5. Contingency planning. if a risk event occurs, what will you do?

6. During which stage of Risk planning are modeling techniques used to determine overall effects of risks on Risks Dashboard project objectives for high probability, high impact risks?

7. What will be the pressing issues of tomorrow?

8. Who is involved in each phase?

9. Did the Risks Dashboard project team have the right skills?

10. When will the Risks Dashboard project be done?

11. What business situation is being addressed?

12. When are the deliverables to be generated in each phase?

13. Will the Risks Dashboard project meet the client requirements, and will it achieve the business success criteria that justified doing the Risks Dashboard project in the first place?

14. Based on your Risks Dashboard project communication management plan, what worked well?

15. Have you evaluated the teams performance and asked for feedback?

16. Measurable - are the targets measurable?

17. Who is performing the work of the Risks Dashboard project?

18. Were resources available as planned?

19. When must it be done?

20. Were decisions made in a timely manner?

1.1 Project Charter: Risks Dashboard

21. Why the improvements?

22. How high should you set your goals?

23. What is the justification?

24. Where and how does the team fit within your organization structure?

25. Who manages integration?

26. What goes into your Risks Dashboard project Charter?

27. Who ise input and support will this Risks Dashboard project require?

28. Strategic fit: what is the strategic initiative identifier for this Risks Dashboard project?

29. Success determination factors: how will the success of the Risks Dashboard project be determined from the customers perspective?

30. Why use a Risks Dashboard project charter?

31. When?

32. What changes can you make to improve?

33. Who is the Risks Dashboard project Manager?

34. What are the known stakeholder requirements?

35. Why have you chosen the aim you have set forth?

36. Risks Dashboard project background: what is the primary motivation for this Risks Dashboard project?

37. Run it as as a startup?

38. When is a charter needed?

39. What are the assumptions?

40. Customer benefits: what customer requirements does this Risks Dashboard project address?

1.2 Stakeholder Register: Risks Dashboard

41. How big is the gap?

42. What & Why?

43. What is the power of the stakeholder?

44. How will reports be created?

45. Who is managing stakeholder engagement?

46. How much influence do they have on the Risks Dashboard project?

47. Who are the stakeholders?

48. Who wants to talk about Security?

49. How should employers make voices heard?

50. Is your organization ready for change?

51. What are the major Risks Dashboard project milestones requiring communications or providing communications opportunities?

52. What opportunities exist to provide communications?

1.3 Stakeholder Analysis Matrix: Risks Dashboard

53. It developments?

54. Identify the stakeholders levels most frequently used –or at least sought– in your Risks Dashboard projects and for which purpose?

55. Vital contracts and partners?

56. Who has control over whom?

57. Where are the good opportunities facing your organizations development?

58. Are you going to weigh the stakeholders?

59. Who influences whom?

60. What do your organizations stakeholders do better than anyone else?

61. What is your Risk Management?

62. Resources, assets, people?

63. Vulnerable groups; who are the vulnerable groups that might be affected by the Risks Dashboard project?

64. What makes a person a stakeholder?

65. Who will be affected by the work?

66. Which conditions out of the control of the management are crucial to contribute for the achievement of the development objective?

67. Is there evidence that demonstrates the impact of education on the Risks Dashboard projects outcomes?

68. Market developments?

69. Who determines value?

70. How much do resources cost?

71. Continuity, supply chain robustness?

2.0 Planning Process Group: Risks Dashboard

72. Just how important is your work to the overall success of the Risks Dashboard project?

73. If a task is partitionable, is this a sufficient condition to reduce the Risks Dashboard project duration?

74. Is the pace of implementing the products of the program ensuring the completeness of the results of the Risks Dashboard project?

75. Product breakdown structure (pbs): what is the Risks Dashboard project result or product, and how should it look like, what are its parts?

76. The Risks Dashboard project charter is created in which Risks Dashboard project management process group?

77. Why is it important to determine activity sequencing on Risks Dashboard projects?

78. Why do it Risks Dashboard projects fail?

79. How will it affect you?

80. Is the identification of the problems, inequalities and gaps, with respective causes, clear in the Risks Dashboard project?

81. Will the products created live up to the necessary quality?

82. What good practices or successful experiences or transferable examples have been identified?

83. Are you just doing busywork to pass the time?

84. How should needs be met?

85. Are work methodologies, financial instruments, etc. shared among departments, organizations and Risks Dashboard projects?

86. Are the necessary foundations in place to ensure the sustainability of the results of the Risks Dashboard project?

87. To what extent do the intervention objectives and strategies of the Risks Dashboard project respond to your organizations plans?

88. Do the partners have sufficient financial capacity to keep up the benefits produced by the programme?

89. What is the difference between the early schedule and late schedule?

2.1 Project Management Plan: Risks Dashboard

90. Are comparable cost estimates used for comparing, screening and selecting alternative plans, and has a reasonable cost estimate been developed for the recommended plan?

91. Is the appropriate plan selected based on your organizations objectives and evaluation criteria expressed in Principles and Guidelines policies?

92. What happened during the process that you found interesting?

93. Does the implementation plan have an appropriate division of responsibilities?

94. Are calculations and results of analyzes essentially correct?

95. If the Risks Dashboard project is complex or scope is specialized, do you have appropriate and/or qualified staff available to perform the tasks?

96. What should you drop in order to add something new?

97. When is a Risks Dashboard project management plan created?

98. Is the engineering content at a feasibility level-of-detail, and is it sufficiently complete, to provide an

adequate basis for the baseline cost estimate?

99. Are there non-structural buyout or relocation recommendations?

100. Did the planning effort collaborate to develop solutions that integrate expertise, policies, programs, and Risks Dashboard projects across entities?

101. Who is the Risks Dashboard project Manager?

102. What goes into your Risks Dashboard project Charter?

103. Who is the sponsor?

104. What is risk management?

105. Are there any windfall benefits that would accrue to the Risks Dashboard project sponsor or other parties?

106. Are there any client staffing expectations?

107. Are the existing and future without-plan conditions reasonable and appropriate?

2.2 Scope Management Plan: Risks Dashboard

108. Is stakeholder involvement adequate?

109. Is there an onboarding process in place?

110. Where do scope management processes fit in?

111. Has appropriate allowance been made for the effect of the learning curve on all personnel joining the Risks Dashboard project who do not have the required prior industry, functional & technical expertise?

112. Does the resource management plan include a personnel development plan?

113. How difficult will it be to do specific activities on this Risks Dashboard project?

114. The greatest degree of uncertainty is encountered during which phase of the Risks Dashboard project life cycle?

115. Is there any form of automated support for Issues Management?

116. Are metrics used to evaluate and manage Vendors?

117. Has the business need been clearly defined?

118. Without-plan conditions?

119. Are tasks tracked by hours?

120. Are estimating assumptions and constraints captured?

121. What are the acceptance criteria (process and criteria to be met for key stakeholder acceptance) and who is authorized to sign off?

122. Are multiple estimation methods being employed?

123. Are the schedule estimates reasonable given the Risks Dashboard project?

124. Assess the expected stability of the scope of this Risks Dashboard project how likely is it to change, how frequently, and by how much?

125. Is it possible to track all classes of Risks Dashboard project work (e.g. scheduled, un-scheduled, defect repair, etc.)?

126. Does the Risks Dashboard project have a Statement of Work?

127. Deliverables -are the deliverables tangible and verifiable?

2.3 Requirements Management Plan: Risks Dashboard

128. Do you expect stakeholders to be cooperative?

129. Subject to change control?

130. Who is responsible for monitoring and tracking the Risks Dashboard project requirements?

131. Will you have access to stakeholders when you need them?

132. How knowledgeable is the team in the proposed application area?

133. When and how will a requirements baseline be established in this Risks Dashboard project?

134. After the requirements are gathered and set forth on the requirements register, theyre little more than a laundry list of items. Some may be duplicates, some might conflict with others and some will be too broad or too vague to understand. Describe how the requirements will be analyzed. Who will perform the analysis?

135. How will bidders price evaluations be done, by deliverables, phases, or in a big bang?

136. Who will perform the analysis?

137. Have stakeholders been instructed in the Change

Control process?

138. Should you include sub-activities?

139. Is the change control process documented?

140. Do you have an agreed upon process for alerting the Risks Dashboard project Manager if a request for change in requirements leads to a product scope change?

141. Is the user satisfied?

142. Could inaccurate or incomplete requirements in this Risks Dashboard project create a serious risk for the business?

143. Do you know which stakeholders will participate in the requirements effort?

144. Who will finally present the work or product(s) for acceptance?

145. How will the information be distributed?

146. Will the contractors involved take full responsibility?

147. Do you have an appropriate arrangement for meetings?

2.4 Requirements Documentation: Risks Dashboard

148. Can you check system requirements?

149. What facilities must be supported by the system?

150. If applicable; are there issues linked with the fact that this is an offshore Risks Dashboard project?

151. How will the proposed Risks Dashboard project help?

152. What if the system wasn t implemented?

153. Is the requirement properly understood?

154. Does the system provide the functions which best support the customers needs?

155. What is your Elevator Speech?

156. Where do system and software requirements come from, what are sources?

157. Where are business rules being captured?

158. Consistency. are there any requirements conflicts?

159. Has requirements gathering uncovered information that would necessitate changes?

160. What is the risk associated with cost and schedule?

161. What marketing channels do you want to use: e-mail, letter or sms?

162. How to document system requirements?

163. What are the attributes of a customer?

164. How linear / iterative is your Requirements Gathering process (or will it be)?

165. What happens when requirements are wrong?

166. How does the proposed Risks Dashboard project contribute to the overall objectives of your organization?

167. Where do you define what is a customer, what are the attributes of customer?

2.5 Requirements Traceability Matrix: Risks Dashboard

168. How do you manage scope?

169. What are the chronologies, contingencies, consequences, criteria?

170. Do you have a clear understanding of all subcontracts in place?

171. How will it affect the stakeholders personally in career?

172. Describe the process for approving requirements so they can be added to the traceability matrix and Risks Dashboard project work can be performed. Will the Risks Dashboard project requirements become approved in writing?

173. Is there a requirements traceability process in place?

174. How small is small enough?

175. What is the WBS?

176. Why do you manage scope?

177. Why use a WBS?

178. What percentage of Risks Dashboard projects are producing traceability matrices between

requirements and other work products?

179. Will you use a Requirements Traceability Matrix?

2.6 Project Scope Statement: Risks Dashboard

180. Are there issues that could affect the existing requirements for the result, service, or product if the scope changes?

181. Will all tasks resulting from issues be entered into the Risks Dashboard project Plan and tracked through the plan?

182. If the scope changes, what will the impact be to your Risks Dashboard project in terms of duration, cost, quality, or any other important areas of the Risks Dashboard project?

183. Did your Risks Dashboard project ask for this?

184. Will the Risks Dashboard project risks be managed according to the Risks Dashboard projects risk management process?

185. Will the risk plan be updated on a regular and frequent basis?

186. Has a method and process for requirement tracking been developed?

187. Does the scope statement still need some clarity?

188. Will an issue form be in use?

189. Relevant - ask yourself can you get there; why are

you doing this Risks Dashboard project?

190. Is the Risks Dashboard project sponsor function identified and defined?

191. Elements that deal with providing the detail?

192. Will the risk status be reported to management on a regular and frequent basis?

193. Any new risks introduced or old risks impacted. Are there issues that could affect the existing requirements for the result, service, or product if the scope changes?

194. Elements of scope management that deal with concept development ?

195. What is the product of this Risks Dashboard project?

196. Is the Risks Dashboard project organization documented and on file?

197. Will this process be communicated to the customer and Risks Dashboard project team?

198. Who will you recommend approve the change, and when do you recommend the change reviews occur?

2.7 Assumption and Constraint Log: Risks Dashboard

199. Are there standards for code development?

200. Is the process working, and people are not executing in compliance of the process?

201. No superfluous information or marketing narrative?

202. Are there procedures in place to effectively manage interdependencies with other Risks Dashboard projects / systems?

203. Is there documentation of system capability requirements, data requirements, environment requirements, security requirements, and computer and hardware requirements?

204. What do you log?

205. Is staff trained on the software technologies that are being used on the Risks Dashboard project?

206. Were the system requirements formally reviewed prior to initiating the design phase?

207. How relevant is this attribute to this Risks Dashboard project or audit?

208. Is the current scope of the Risks Dashboard project substantially different than that originally

defined in the approved Risks Dashboard project plan?

209. What strengths do you have?

210. Is this model reasonable?

211. Are there unnecessary steps that are creating bottlenecks and/or causing people to wait?

212. Was the document/deliverable developed per the appropriate or required standards (for example, Institute of Electrical and Electronics Engineers standards)?

213. Are there processes defining how software will be developed including development methods, overall timeline for development, software product standards, and traceability?

214. How are new requirements or changes to requirements identified?

215. Should factors be unpredictable over time?

216. Do the requirements meet the standards of correctness, completeness, consistency, accuracy, and readability?

217. What weaknesses do you have?

2.8 Work Breakdown Structure: Risks Dashboard

218. When does it have to be done?

219. Is it still viable?

220. Do you need another level?

221. How much detail?

222. When do you stop?

223. What is the probability of completing the Risks Dashboard project in less that xx days?

224. What has to be done?

225. How will you and your Risks Dashboard project team define the Risks Dashboard projects scope and work breakdown structure?

226. How big is a work-package?

227. Is it a change in scope?

228. Where does it take place?

229. Why would you develop a Work Breakdown Structure?

230. Can you make it?

231. When would you develop a Work Breakdown Structure?

232. Who has to do it?

233. Is the work breakdown structure (wbs) defined and is the scope of the Risks Dashboard project clear with assigned deliverable owners?

234. Why is it useful?

235. How far down?

2.9 WBS Dictionary: Risks Dashboard

236. Does the scheduling system identify in a timely manner the status of work?

237. Are overhead cost budgets (or Risks Dashboard projections) established on a facility-wide basis at least annually for the life of the contract?

238. How many levels?

239. Is subcontracted work defined and identified to the appropriate subcontractor within the proper WBS element?

240. Are Risks Dashboard projected overhead costs in each pool and the associated direct costs used as the basis for establishing interim rates for allocating overhead to contracts?

241. Is cost and schedule performance measurement done in a consistent, systematic manner?

242. Are retroactive changes to direct costs and indirect costs prohibited except for the correction of errors and routine accounting adjustments?

243. Should you have a test for each code module?

244. Does the contractors system provide for the determination of cost variances attributable to the excess usage of material?

245. Are material costs reported within the same

period as that in which BCWP is earned for that material?

246. Identify potential or actual overruns and underruns?

247. Are all authorized tasks assigned to identified organizational elements?

248. What is the end result of a work package?

249. Does the cost accumulation system provide for summarization of indirect costs from the point of allocation to the contract total?

250. Do work packages reflect the actual way in which the work will be done and are they meaningful products or management-oriented subdivisions of a higher level element of work?

251. Are the rates for allocating costs from each indirect cost pool to contracts updated as necessary to ensure a realistic monthly allocation of indirect costs without significant year-end adjustments?

252. Are records maintained to show how management reserves are used?

253. What size should a work package be?

254. Wbs elements contractually specified for reporting of status to you (lowest level only)?

255. The total budget for the contract (including estimates for authorized and unpriced work)?

2.10 Schedule Management Plan: Risks Dashboard

256. Do all stakeholders know how to access this repository and where to find the Risks Dashboard project documentation?

257. Is there general agreement & acceptance of the current status and progress of the Risks Dashboard project?

258. Timeline and milestones?

259. Are vendor contract reports, reviews and visits conducted periodically?

260. Are trade-offs between accepting the risk and mitigating the risk identified?

261. Who is responsible for estimating the activity durations?

262. Have key stakeholders been identified?

263. Is a process defined to measure the performance of the schedule management process itself?

264. How do you manage time?

265. Are the schedule estimates reasonable given the Risks Dashboard project?

266. Is there a formal set of procedures supporting

Stakeholder Management?

267. Has a provision been made to reassess Risks Dashboard project risks at various Risks Dashboard project stages?

268. Is your organization certified as a supplier, wholesaler and/or regular dealer?

269. Are meeting minutes captured and sent out after the meeting?

270. Is a process for scheduling and reporting defined, including forms and formats?

271. What will be the final cost of the Risks Dashboard project if status quo is maintained?

2.11 Activity List: Risks Dashboard

272. Who will perform the work?

273. Is there anything planned that does not need to be here?

274. What are the critical bottleneck activities?

275. What went right?

276. How can the Risks Dashboard project be displayed graphically to better visualize the activities?

277. How should ongoing costs be monitored to try to keep the Risks Dashboard project within budget?

278. When do the individual activities need to start and finish?

279. What is the total time required to complete the Risks Dashboard project if no delays occur?

280. Are the required resources available or need to be acquired?

281. What is the LF and LS for each activity?

282. In what sequence?

283. Where will it be performed?

284. For other activities, how much delay can be tolerated?

285. Is infrastructure setup part of your Risks Dashboard project?

286. What went well?

287. What will be performed?

288. What did not go as well?

289. What is your organizations history in doing similar activities?

290. How difficult will it be to do specific activities on this Risks Dashboard project?

2.12 Activity Attributes: Risks Dashboard

291. How many resources do you need to complete the work scope within a limit of X number of days?

292. How much activity detail is required?

293. Activity: fair or not fair?

294. Where else does it apply?

295. Has management defined a definite timeframe for the turnaround or Risks Dashboard project window?

296. How difficult will it be to complete specific activities on this Risks Dashboard project?

297. Resources to accomplish the work?

298. What conclusions/generalizations can you draw from this?

299. How many days do you need to complete the work scope with a limit of X number of resources?

300. Were there other ways you could have organized the data to achieve similar results?

301. Why?

302. How else could the items be grouped?

303. How difficult will it be to do specific activities on this Risks Dashboard project?

304. What activity do you think you should spend the most time on?

305. Have you identified the Activity Leveling Priority code value on each activity?

306. Are the required resources available?

307. Does your organization of the data change its meaning?

2.13 Milestone List: Risks Dashboard

308. Describe the industry you are in and the market growth opportunities. What is the market for your technology, product or service?

309. Calculate how long can activity be delayed?

310. Usps (unique selling points)?

311. Do you foresee any technical risks or developmental challenges?

312. What date will the task finish?

313. Loss of key staff?

314. How late can each activity be finished and started?

315. Information and research?

316. Describe the concept of the technology, product or service that will be or has been developed. How will it be used?

317. Sustaining internal capabilities?

318. It is to be a narrative text providing the crucial aspects of your Risks Dashboard project proposal answering what, who, how, when and where?

319. Who will manage the Risks Dashboard project on a day-to-day basis?

320. Marketing - reach, distribution, awareness?

321. How late can the activity finish?

322. How will the milestone be verified?

323. Global influences?

324. Describe your organizations strengths and core competencies. What factors will make your organization succeed?

325. What has been done so far?

326. New USPs?

2.14 Network Diagram: Risks Dashboard

327. Planning: who, how long, what to do?

328. What is the probability of completing the Risks Dashboard project in less that xx days?

329. Where do you schedule uncertainty time?

330. What is the completion time?

331. What controls the start and finish of a job?

332. What are the tools?

333. What are the Key Success Factors?

334. What job or jobs precede it?

335. Can you calculate the confidence level?

336. Which type of network diagram allows you to depict four types of dependencies?

337. If the Risks Dashboard project network diagram cannot change and you have extra personnel resources, what is the BEST thing to do?

338. Are the gantt chart and/or network diagram updated periodically and used to assess the overall Risks Dashboard project timetable?

339. What is the lowest cost to complete this Risks Dashboard project in xx weeks?

340. What activities must occur simultaneously with this activity?

341. Where do schedules come from?

342. Exercise: what is the probability that the Risks Dashboard project duration will exceed xx weeks?

343. If a current contract exists, can you provide the vendor name, contract start, and contract expiration date?

344. What job or jobs could run concurrently?

345. What must be completed before an activity can be started?

2.15 Activity Resource Requirements: Risks Dashboard

346. What is the Work Plan Standard?

347. Anything else?

348. How many signatures do you require on a check and does this match what is in your policy and procedures?

349. What are constraints that you might find during the Human Resource Planning process?

350. Organizational Applicability?

351. When does monitoring begin?

352. Time for overtime?

353. Do you use tools like decomposition and rolling-wave planning to produce the activity list and other outputs?

354. Other support in specific areas?

355. Are there unresolved issues that need to be addressed?

356. How do you handle petty cash?

357. Why do you do that?

358. Which logical relationship does the PDM use most often?

2.16 Resource Breakdown Structure: Risks Dashboard

359. Who will use the system?

360. What defines a successful Risks Dashboard project?

361. What is each stakeholders desired outcome for the Risks Dashboard project?

362. What went wrong?

363. The list could probably go on, but, the thing that you would most like to know is, How long & How much?

364. How should the information be delivered?

365. Goals for the Risks Dashboard project. What is each stakeholders desired outcome for the Risks Dashboard project?

366. What is the purpose of assigning and documenting responsibility?

367. What is Risks Dashboard project communication management?

368. Which resources should be in the resource pool?

369. Changes based on input from stakeholders?

370. What is the primary purpose of the human resource plan?

371. Who delivers the information?

372. Any changes from stakeholders?

373. Who is allowed to perform which functions?

374. How difficult will it be to do specific activities on this Risks Dashboard project?

375. Why do you do it?

2.17 Activity Duration Estimates: Risks Dashboard

376. Are activity duration estimates documented?

377. How is the Risks Dashboard project doing?

378. What are the Risks Dashboard project management deliverables of each process group?

379. Do Risks Dashboard project team members work in the same physical location to enhance team performance?

380. Do checklists exist that list frequently performed activities?

381. What functions does this software provide that cannot be done easily using other tools such as a spreadsheet or database?

382. How can software assist in Risks Dashboard project communications?

383. Which frame seemed to be the most important and why?

384. Are team building activities completed to improve team performance?

385. Does a process exist to determine the probability of risk events?

386. What are the main types of goods and services being outsourced?

387. Are costs that may be needed to account for Risks Dashboard project risks determined?

388. Which is correct?

389. Account for the make-or-buy process and how to perform the financial calculations involved in the process. What are the main types of contracts if you do decide to outsource?

390. How does the job market and current state of the economy affect human resource management?

391. Given your research into similar classes and the work you think is required for this Risks Dashboard project, what assumptions, variables, or costs would you change from the information provided above?

392. How can others help Risks Dashboard project managers understand your organizational context for Risks Dashboard projects?

393. What are the main types of contracts if you do decide to outsource?

2.18 Duration Estimating Worksheet: Risks Dashboard

394. What is cost and Risks Dashboard project cost management?

395. How should ongoing costs be monitored to try to keep the Risks Dashboard project within budget?

396. Small or large Risks Dashboard project?

397. Is this operation cost effective?

398. Is the Risks Dashboard project responsive to community need?

399. Does the Risks Dashboard project provide innovative ways for stakeholders to overcome obstacles or deliver better outcomes?

400. Do any colleagues have experience with your organization and/or RFPs?

401. What utility impacts are there?

402. Can the Risks Dashboard project be constructed as planned?

403. What work will be included in the Risks Dashboard project?

404. What questions do you have?

405. Is a construction detail attached (to aid in explanation)?

406. Done before proceeding with this activity or what can be done concurrently?

407. What is the total time required to complete the Risks Dashboard project if no delays occur?

408. Why estimate time and cost?

409. How can the Risks Dashboard project be displayed graphically to better visualize the activities?

410. What is your role?

411. Science = process: remember the scientific method?

2.19 Project Schedule: Risks Dashboard

412. Are key risk mitigation strategies added to the Risks Dashboard project schedule?

413. How can you fix it?

414. Did the final product meet or exceed user expectations?

415. Eliminate unnecessary activities. Are there activities that came from a template or previous Risks Dashboard project that are not applicable on this phase of this Risks Dashboard project?

416. Are activities connected because logic dictates the order in which others occur?

417. Activity charts and bar charts are graphical representations of a Risks Dashboard project schedule ...how do they differ?

418. Your best shot for providing estimations how complex/how much work does the activity require?

419. Did the Risks Dashboard project come in on schedule?

420. How can you address that situation?

421. How can you shorten the schedule?

422. Did the Risks Dashboard project come in under budget?

423. Understand the constraints used in preparing the schedule. Are activities connected because logic dictates the order in which others occur?

424. How does a Risks Dashboard project get to be a year late ?

425. Are all remaining durations correct?

426. How detailed should a Risks Dashboard project get?

427. Schedule/cost recovery?

428. What does that mean?

429. Master Risks Dashboard project schedule?

430. What is risk?

2.20 Cost Management Plan: Risks Dashboard

431. Are enough systems & user personnel assigned to the Risks Dashboard project?

432. Are mitigation strategies identified?

433. Forecasts – how will the time and resources needed to complete the Risks Dashboard project be forecast?

434. Are decisions captured in a decisions log?

435. Does the schedule include Risks Dashboard project management time and change request analysis time?

436. Are target dates established for each milestone deliverable?

437. Is there a formal set of procedures supporting Issues Management?

438. Are Risks Dashboard project team members involved in detailed estimating and scheduling?

439. Is it a Risks Dashboard project?

440. Published materials?

441. Are any non-compliance issues that exist due to State practices communicated to your organization?

442. What would the life cycle costs be?

443. Cost estimate preparation – What cost estimates will be prepared during the Risks Dashboard project phases?

444. Vac -variance at completion, how much over/ under budget do you expect to be?

445. Is a pmo (Risks Dashboard project management office) in place and provide oversight to the Risks Dashboard project?

446. Are cause and effect determined for risks when others occur?

447. Personnel with expertise?

448. Are issues raised, assessed, actioned, and resolved in a timely and efficient manner?

2.21 Activity Cost Estimates: Risks Dashboard

449. Were escalated issues resolved promptly?

450. Did the consultant work with local staff to develop local capacity?

451. How do you manage cost?

452. What do you want to know about the stay to know if costs were inappropriately high or low?

453. What is your organizations history in doing similar tasks?

454. What is the last item a Risks Dashboard project manager must do to finalize Risks Dashboard project close-out?

455. How many activities should you have?

456. How do you fund change orders?

457. What are you looking for?

458. Will you use any tools, such as Risks Dashboard project management software, to assist in capturing Earned Value metrics?

459. Is there anything unique in this Risks Dashboard projects scope statement that will affect resources?

460. Does the activity serve a common type of customer?

461. Who determines when the contractor is paid?

462. Were you satisfied with the work?

463. How Award?

464. Based on your Risks Dashboard project communication management plan, what worked well?

465. What makes a good expected result statement?

466. What makes a good activity description?

467. What defines a successful Risks Dashboard project?

468. How and when do you enter into Risks Dashboard project Procurement Management?

2.22 Cost Estimating Worksheet: Risks Dashboard

469. What will others want?

470. Does the Risks Dashboard project provide innovative ways for stakeholders to overcome obstacles or deliver better outcomes?

471. Is the Risks Dashboard project responsive to community need?

472. What is the estimated labor cost today based upon this information?

473. Identify the timeframe necessary to monitor progress and collect data to determine how the selected measure has changed?

474. What happens to any remaining funds not used?

475. What info is needed?

476. What additional Risks Dashboard project(s) could be initiated as a result of this Risks Dashboard project?

477. Will the Risks Dashboard project collaborate with the local community and leverage resources?

478. Is it feasible to establish a control group arrangement?

479. How will the results be shared and to whom?

480. What costs are to be estimated?

481. Value pocket identification & quantification what are value pockets?

482. What is the purpose of estimating?

483. Can a trend be established from historical performance data on the selected measure and are the criteria for using trend analysis or forecasting methods met?

484. Who is best positioned to know and assist in identifying corresponding factors?

485. Ask: are others positioned to know, are others credible, and will others cooperate?

486. What can be included?

2.23 Cost Baseline: Risks Dashboard

487. Have all approved changes to the schedule baseline been identified and impact on the Risks Dashboard project documented?

488. What threats might prevent you from getting there?

489. Is the requested change request a result of changes in other Risks Dashboard project(s)?

490. What is the reality?

491. What is the most important thing to do next to make your Risks Dashboard project successful?

492. How concrete were original objectives?

493. Does the suggested change request represent a desired enhancement to the products functionality?

494. Have the lessons learned been filed with the Risks Dashboard project Management Office?

495. What is the consequence?

496. Does the suggested change request seem to represent a necessary enhancement to the product?

497. Does it impact schedule, cost, quality?

498. Why do you manage cost?

499. Are you meeting with your team regularly?

500. Are there contingencies or conditions related to the acceptance?

501. Has the actual cost of the Risks Dashboard project (or Risks Dashboard project phase) been tallied and compared to the approved budget?

502. What do you want to measure ?

2.24 Quality Management Plan: Risks Dashboard

503. How is staff trained on the recording of field notes?

504. Are formal code reviews conducted?

505. What is the Difference Between a QMP and QAPP?

506. Does the Risks Dashboard project have a formal Risks Dashboard project Plan?

507. Is the steering committee active in Risks Dashboard project oversight?

508. Meet how often?

509. Are there processes in place to ensure internal consistency between the source code components?

510. What would you gain if you spent time working to improve this process?

511. Does the system design reflect the requirements?

512. What are your results for key measures/indicators of accomplishment of organizational strategy?

513. How are changes to procedures made?

514. Are there nonconformance issues?

515. What are your organizations current levels and trends for the already stated measures related to customer satisfaction/ dissatisfaction and product/ service performance?

516. How are changes approved?

517. What are the established criteria that sampling / testing data are compared against?

518. How do you ensure that protocols are up to date?

519. Can the requirements be traced to the appropriate components of the solution, as well as test scripts?

520. What is quality planning ?

521. How are records kept in the office?

522. What is positive about the current process?

2.25 Quality Metrics: Risks Dashboard

523. When is the security analysis testing complete?

524. Is there a set of procedures to capture, analyze and act on quality metrics?

525. How do you communicate results and findings to upper management?

526. Which data do others need in one place to target areas of improvement?

527. When will the Final Guidance will be issued?

528. Is quality culture a competitive advantage?

529. What documentation is required?

530. Which are the right metrics to use?

531. How effective are your security tests?

532. How can the effectiveness of each of the activities be measured?

533. What percentage are outcome-based?

534. How are requirements conflicts resolved?

535. What is the timeline to meet your goal?

536. Have alternatives been defined in the event that failure occurs?

537. Filter visualizations of interest?

538. What if the biggest risk to your business were the already stated people who do not complain?

539. What is the benchmark?

540. What method of measurement do you use?

541. What happens if you get an abnormal result?

2.26 Process Improvement Plan: Risks Dashboard

542. What is the return on investment?

543. Where are you now?

544. Where do you focus?

545. If a process improvement framework is being used, which elements will help the problems and goals listed?

546. Purpose of goal: the motive is determined by asking, why do you want to achieve this goal?

547. Where do you want to be?

548. Are you making progress on the improvement framework?

549. What personnel are the champions for the initiative?

550. To elicit goal statements, do you ask a question such as, What do you want to achieve?

551. Who should prepare the process improvement action plan?

552. Are you making progress on the goals?

553. Does explicit definition of the measures exist?

554. What is the test-cycle concept?

555. Has a process guide to collect the data been developed?

556. Have the supporting tools been developed or acquired?

557. The motive is determined by asking, Why do you want to achieve this goal?

558. What lessons have you learned so far?

559. What personnel are the sponsors for that initiative?

560. Are you making progress on your improvement plan?

2.27 Responsibility Assignment Matrix: Risks Dashboard

561. The staff characteristics – is the group or the person capable to work together as a team?

562. Too many as: does a proper segregation of duties exist?

563. The staff interests – is the group or the person interested in working for this Risks Dashboard project?

564. Changes in the overhead pool and/or organization structures?

565. Are indirect costs accumulated for comparison with the corresponding budgets?

566. Not any rs, as, or cs: if an identified role is only informed, should others be eliminated from the matrix?

567. Too many rs: with too many people labeled as doing the work, are there too many hands involved?

568. Time-phased control account budgets?

569. Identify and isolate causes of favorable and unfavorable cost and schedule variances?

570. Is the entire contract planned in time-phased control accounts to the extent practicable?

571. What cost control tool do many experts say is crucial to Risks Dashboard project management?

572. What do you need to implement earned value management?

573. When performing is split among two or more roles, is the work clearly defined so that the efforts are coordinated and the communication is clear?

574. Too many is: do all the identified roles need to be routinely informed or only in exceptional circumstances?

575. Who is going to do that work?

576. Is it safe to say you can handle more work or that some tasks you are supposed to do arent worth doing?

577. Why cost benefit analysis?

2.28 Roles and Responsibilities: Risks Dashboard

578. Is there a training program in place for stakeholders covering expectations, roles and responsibilities and any addition knowledge others need to be good stakeholders?

579. Authority: what areas/Risks Dashboard projects in your work do you have the authority to decide upon and act on the already stated decisions?

580. What specific behaviors did you observe?

581. What should you do now to prepare for your career 5+ years from now?

582. Are governance roles and responsibilities documented?

583. Attainable / achievable: the goal is attainable; can you actually accomplish the goal?

584. What should you do now to prepare yourself for a promotion, increased responsibilities or a different job?

585. Key conclusions and recommendations: Are conclusions and recommendations relevant and acceptable?

586. What is working well?

587. Is the data complete?

588. Who: who is involved?

589. Where are you most strong as a supervisor?

590. What areas of supervision are challenging for you?

591. Influence: what areas of organizational decision making are you able to influence when you do not have authority to make the final decision?

592. Are Risks Dashboard project team roles and responsibilities identified and documented?

593. How well did the Risks Dashboard project Team understand the expectations of specific roles and responsibilities?

594. Are the quality assurance functions and related roles and responsibilities clearly defined?

595. Who is involved?

2.29 Human Resource Management Plan: Risks Dashboard

596. What areas does the group agree are the biggest success on the Risks Dashboard project?

597. How relevant is this attribute to this Risks Dashboard project or audit?

598. Is there an issues management plan in place?

599. Are all key components of a Quality Assurance Plan present?

600. Are action items captured and managed?

601. Are the payment terms being followed?

602. Is pert / critical path or equivalent methodology being used?

603. Are all vendor contracts closed out?

604. How to convince to employees that it is a necessary process?

605. What communication items need improvement?

606. List roles. what commitments have been made?

607. Has a capability assessment been conducted?

608. Are risk triggers captured?

609. What is the boss?

610. Were stakeholders aware and supportive of the principles and practices of modern cost estimation?

611. Are adequate resources provided for the quality assurance function?

2.30 Communications Management Plan: Risks Dashboard

612. Why manage stakeholders?

613. Who needs to know and how much?

614. How will the person responsible for executing the communication item be notified?

615. Are there too many who have an interest in some aspect of your work?

616. Who are the members of the governing body?

617. Will messages be directly related to the release strategy or phases of the Risks Dashboard project?

618. Who to learn from?

619. Are others needed?

620. Are the stakeholders getting the information others need, are others consulted, are concerns addressed?

621. In your work, how much time is spent on stakeholder identification?

622. What is the stakeholders level of authority?

623. Do you prepare stakeholder engagement plans?

624. What are the interrelationships?

625. Conflict resolution -which method when?

626. What is Risks Dashboard project communications management?

627. What to know?

628. What approaches do you use?

629. Can you think of other people who might have concerns or interests?

630. Where do team members get information?

631. What help do you and your team need from the stakeholder?

2.31 Risk Management Plan: Risks Dashboard

632. Which risks should get the attention?

633. Can the Risks Dashboard project proceed without assuming the risk?

634. Monitoring -what factors can you track that will enable you to determine if the risk is becoming more or less likely?

635. Prioritized components/features?

636. How quickly does each item need to be resolved?

637. What is the probability the risk avoidance strategy will be successful?

638. What things might go wrong?

639. Who has experience with this?

640. Why might it be late?

641. Where are you confronted with risks during the business phases?

642. Risks should be identified during which phase of Risks Dashboard project management life cycle?

643. Does the customer understand the software process?

644. What will the damage be?

645. Do the people have the right combinations of skills?

646. For software; does the software interface with new or unproven hardware or unproven vendor products?

647. Are there alternative opinions/solutions/ processes you should explore?

648. Are enough people available?

649. Are status updates being made on schedule and are the updates clearly described?

650. Are the reports useful and easy to read?

651. Are testing tools available and suitable?

2.32 Risk Register: Risks Dashboard

652. Can the likelihood and impact of failing to achieve corresponding recommendations and action plans be assessed?

653. Schedule impact/severity estimated range (workdays) assume the event happens, what is the potential impact?

654. Have other controls and solutions been implemented in other services which could be applied as an alternative to additional funding?

655. Are implemented controls working as others should?

656. What may happen or not go according to plan?

657. Is further information required before making a decision?

658. Do you require further engagement?

659. What is the reason for current performance gaps and do the risks and opportunities identified previously account for this?

660. What are your key risks/show istoppers and what is being done to manage them?

661. Which key risks have ineffective responses or outstanding improvement actions?

662. Amongst the action plans and recommendations that you have to introduce are there some that could stop or delay the overall program?

663. What would the impact to the Risks Dashboard project objectives be should the risk arise?

664. Manageability – have mitigations to the risk been identified?

665. What further options might be available for responding to the risk?

666. Are there any knock-on effects/impact on any of the other areas?

667. Severity Prediction?

668. What risks might negatively or positively affect achieving the Risks Dashboard project objectives?

669. Contingency actions - planned actions to reduce the immediate seriousness of the risk when it does occur. What should you do when?

670. Having taken action, how did the responses effect change, and where is the Risks Dashboard project now?

671. How often will the Risk Management Plan and Risk Register be formally reviewed, and by whom?

2.33 Probability and Impact Assessment: Risks Dashboard

672. Are the software tools integrated with each other?

673. Is there additional information that would make you more confident about your analysis?

674. Are formal technical reviews part of this process?

675. What action do you usually take against risks?

676. Do you use diagramming techniques to show cause and effect?

677. Workarounds are determined during which step of risk management?

678. What are the current or emerging trends of culture?

679. How well is the risk understood?

680. What are the current demands of the customer?

681. What would be the effect of slippage?

682. Costs associated with late delivery or a defective product?

683. Is the customer willing to commit significant time to the requirements gathering process?

684. What is the impact if the risk does occur?

685. Is the customer willing to participate in reviews?

686. Who will be in command to monitor and control the performance of the consortium members (consortium leader/client)?

687. Has something like this been done before?

688. Have you ascribed a level of confidence to every critical technical objective?

689. Can you avoid altogether some things that might go wrong?

690. How do risks change during a Risks Dashboard project life cycle?

2.34 Probability and Impact Matrix: Risks Dashboard

691. Maximize short-term return on investment?

692. What is the level of commitment and professionalism?

693. While preparing your risk responses, you identify additional risks. What should you do?

694. How to prioritize risks?

695. Is the number of people on the Risks Dashboard project team adequate to do the job?

696. Is there any sign of biased ranking?

697. During which risk management process is a determination to transfer a risk made?

698. Lay ground work for future returns?

699. Which is the BEST thing to do?

700. What things are likely to change?

701. Were there any Risks Dashboard projects similar to this one in existence?

702. What should you do FIRST?

703. Do requirements demand the use of new

analysis, design, or testing methods?

704. What can you use the analyzed risks for?

705. What will be the likely incidence of conflict with neighboring Risks Dashboard projects?

706. Do the requirements require the creation of new algorithms?

707. Mandated specific features?

708. Can it be changed quickly?

709. Which phase of the Risks Dashboard project do you take part in?

2.35 Risk Data Sheet: Risks Dashboard

710. What will be the consequences if it happens?

711. Has the most cost-effective solution been chosen?

712. How do you handle product safely?

713. Are new hazards created?

714. What are the main threats to your existence?

715. Has a sensitivity analysis been carried out?

716. How can it happen?

717. Risk of what?

718. What is the chance that it will happen?

719. What actions can be taken to eliminate or remove risk?

720. During work activities could hazards exist?

721. What is the likelihood of it happening?

722. Whom do you serve (customers)?

723. What are your core values?

724. What are you trying to achieve (Objectives)?

725. What are you weak at and therefore need to do better?

726. What can happen?

727. What was measured?

728. Who has a vested interest in how you perform as your organization (our stakeholders)?

2.36 Procurement Management Plan: Risks Dashboard

729. Are actuals compared against estimates to analyze and correct variances?

730. Is it possible to track all classes of Risks Dashboard project work (e.g. scheduled, un-scheduled, defect repair, etc.)?

731. How and when do you enter into Risks Dashboard project Procurement Management?

732. What are you trying to accomplish?

733. Are the people assigned to the Risks Dashboard project sufficiently qualified?

734. Have activity relationships and interdependencies within tasks been adequately identified?

735. Are the appropriate IT resources adequate to meet planned commitments?

736. What were things that you did well, and could improve, and how?

737. Do all stakeholders know how to access the PM repository and where to find the Risks Dashboard project documentation?

738. Has the scope management document been

updated and distributed to help prevent scope creep?

739. Are Risks Dashboard project team members involved in detailed estimating and scheduling?

740. Is the current scope of the Risks Dashboard project substantially different than that originally defined?

741. Have all involved Risks Dashboard project stakeholders and work groups committed to the Risks Dashboard project?

742. Are the Risks Dashboard project plans updated on a frequent basis?

743. Is the communication plan being followed?

744. Does the detailed work plan match the complexity of tasks with the capabilities of personnel?

2.37 Source Selection Criteria: Risks Dashboard

745. How important is cost in the source selection decision relative to past performance and technical considerations?

746. Can you prevent comparison of proposals?

747. Are considerations anticipated?

748. How do you encourage efficiency and consistency?

749. Do you consider all weaknesses, significant weaknesses, and deficiencies?

750. How should oral presentations be prepared for?

751. What information may not be provided?

752. What is cost analysis and when should it be performed?

753. What should clarifications include?

754. What evidence should be provided regarding proposal evaluations?

755. Can you reasonably estimate total organization requirements for the coming year?

756. Who should attend debriefings?

757. Does an evaluation need to include the identification of strengths and weaknesses?

758. What documentation should be used to support the selection decision?

759. What benefits are accrued from issuing a DRFP in advance of issuing a final RFP?

760. Has all proposal data been loaded?

761. What past performance information should be requested?

762. How can solicitation Schedules be improved to yield more effective price competition?

763. How can business terms and conditions be improved to yield more effective price competition?

764. How will you evaluate offerors proposals?

2.38 Stakeholder Management Plan: Risks Dashboard

765. Are schedule deliverables actually delivered?

766. Has a Risks Dashboard project Communications Plan been developed?

767. Are procurement deliverables arriving on time and to specification?

768. Will the current technology alter during the life of the Risks Dashboard project?

769. Is a payment system in place with proper reviews and approvals?

770. Is documentation created for communication with the suppliers and vendors?

771. Are the people assigned to the Risks Dashboard project sufficiently qualified?

772. What specific resources will be required for implementation activities?

773. Have all involved stakeholders and work groups committed to the Risks Dashboard project?

774. Does the Risks Dashboard project have a Quality Culture?

775. Are corrective actions and variances reported?

776. Have the key functions and capabilities been defined and assigned to each release or iteration?

777. Will all relevant stakeholders be included within the review process?

778. Does the role of the Risks Dashboard project Team cease upon the delivery of the Risks Dashboard projects outputs?

779. What is the general purpose in defining responsibilities of the already stated affiliated with the Risks Dashboard project?

2.39 Change Management Plan: Risks Dashboard

780. Have the business unit contacts been selected and notified?

781. How many people are required in each of the roles?

782. What roles within your organization are affected, and how?

783. What did the people around you say about it?

784. What is the worst thing that can happen if you chose not to communicate this information?

785. Which relationships will change?

786. What time commitment will this involve?

787. What are the responsibilities assigned to each role?

788. What are the needs, priorities and special interests of the audience?

789. Is there a support model for this application and are the details available for distribution?

790. Will the culture embrace or reject this change?

791. Have the approved procedures and policies been

published?

792. What is the most positive interpretation it can receive?

793. What are the specific target groups / audience that will be impacted by this change?

794. Has the target training audience been identified and nominated?

795. What method and medium would you use to announce a message?

796. How do you know the requirements you documented are the right ones?

797. Impact of systems implementation on organization change?

798. Who in the business it includes?

3.0 Executing Process Group: Risks Dashboard

799. Why do you need a good WBS to use Risks Dashboard project management software?

800. Who will provide training?

801. When is the appropriate time to bring the scorecard to Board meetings?

802. How do you prevent staff are just doing busywork to pass the time?

803. Could a new application negatively affect the current IT infrastructure?

804. How can software assist in procuring goods and services?

805. If a risk event occurs, what will you do?

806. Is activity definition the first process involved in Risks Dashboard project time management?

807. Is the schedule for the set products being met?

808. What are the typical Risks Dashboard project management skills?

809. Are escalated issues resolved promptly?

810. How does a Risks Dashboard project life cycle

differ from a product life cycle?

811. How can you use Microsoft Risks Dashboard project and Excel to assist in Risks Dashboard project risk management?

812. What type of information goes in the quality assurance plan?

813. What is the shortest possible time it will take to complete this Risks Dashboard project?

814. Mitigate. what will you do to minimize the impact should a risk event occur?

815. After how many days will the lease cost be the same as the purchase cost for the equipment?

816. What were things that you did very well and want to do the same again on the next Risks Dashboard project?

3.1 Team Member Status Report: Risks Dashboard

817. How much risk is involved?

818. Why is it to be done?

819. Does every department have to have a Risks Dashboard project Manager on staff?

820. When a teams productivity and success depend on collaboration and the efficient flow of information, what generally fails them?

821. Are the products of your organizations Risks Dashboard projects meeting customers objectives?

822. How can you make it practical?

823. What is to be done?

824. What specific interest groups do you have in place?

825. Are your organizations Risks Dashboard projects more successful over time?

826. The problem with Reward & Recognition Programs is that the truly deserving people all too often get left out. How can you make it practical?

827. Will the staff do training or is that done by a third party?

828. Do you have an Enterprise Risks Dashboard project Management Office (EPMO)?

829. How does this product, good, or service meet the needs of the Risks Dashboard project and your organization as a whole?

830. How will resource planning be done?

831. Is there evidence that staff is taking a more professional approach toward management of your organizations Risks Dashboard projects?

832. Does the product, good, or service already exist within your organization?

833. Does your organization have the means (staff, money, contract, etc.) to produce or to acquire the product, good, or service?

834. How it is to be done?

835. Are the attitudes of staff regarding Risks Dashboard project work improving?

3.2 Change Request: Risks Dashboard

836. How can changes be graded?

837. Why do you want to have a change control system?

838. What are the Impacts to your organization?

839. For which areas does this operating procedure apply?

840. How well do experienced software developers predict software change?

841. Can you answer what happened, who did it, when did it happen, and what else will be affected?

842. How are changes requested (forms, method of communication)?

843. What has an inspector to inspect and to check?

844. How shall the implementation of changes be recorded?

845. Since there are no change requests in your Risks Dashboard project at this point, what must you have before you begin?

846. How are changes graded and who is responsible for the rating?

847. Who can suggest changes?

848. What needs to be communicated?

849. What mechanism is used to appraise others of changes that are made?

850. How many times must the change be modified or presented to the change control board before it is approved?

851. Will new change requests be acknowledged in a timely manner?

852. Will there be a change request form in use?

853. Should a more thorough impact analysis be conducted?

854. Who is included in the change control team?

855. Have all related configuration items been properly updated?

3.3 Change Log: Risks Dashboard

856. Will the Risks Dashboard project fail if the change request is not executed?

857. Who initiated the change request?

858. When was the request submitted?

859. When was the request approved?

860. Is the change request open, closed or pending?

861. Is the change request within Risks Dashboard project scope?

862. Do the described changes impact on the integrity or security of the system?

863. Is the requested change request a result of changes in other Risks Dashboard project(s)?

864. Is the submitted change a new change or a modification of a previously approved change?

865. How does this relate to the standards developed for specific business processes?

866. Is this a mandatory replacement?

867. How does this change affect scope?

868. How does this change affect the timeline of the schedule?

869. Is the change backward compatible without limitations?

870. Where do changes come from?

3.4 Decision Log: Risks Dashboard

871. Do strategies and tactics aimed at less than full control reduce the costs of management or simply shift the cost burden?

872. Decision-making process; how will the team make decisions?

873. What alternatives/risks were considered?

874. Which variables make a critical difference?

875. At what point in time does loss become unacceptable?

876. How does an increasing emphasis on cost containment influence the strategies and tactics used?

877. Linked to original objective?

878. What makes you different or better than others companies selling the same thing?

879. Who will be given a copy of this document and where will it be kept?

880. Behaviors; what are guidelines that the team has identified that will assist them with getting the most out of team meetings?

881. What is your overall strategy for quality control / quality assurance procedures?

882. Who is the decisionmaker?

883. Is your opponent open to a non-traditional workflow, or will it likely challenge anything you do?

884. With whom was the decision shared or considered?

885. How does the use a Decision Support System influence the strategies/tactics or costs?

886. What was the rationale for the decision?

887. How does provision of information, both in terms of content and presentation, influence acceptance of alternative strategies?

888. What eDiscovery problem or issue did your organization set out to fix or make better?

889. Does anything need to be adjusted?

890. What is the line where eDiscovery ends and document review begins?

3.5 Quality Audit: Risks Dashboard

891. How does your organization know that its research programs are appropriately effective and constructive?

892. How does your organization know that its system for managing intellectual property issues is appropriately effective, constructive and fair?

893. What will the Observer get to Observe?

894. What are you trying to do?

895. How does your organization know that the system for managing its facilities is appropriately effective and constructive?

896. How does your organization know that its processes for managing severance are appropriately effective, constructive and fair?

897. What does an analysis of your organizations staff profile suggest in terms of its planning, and how is this being addressed?

898. What are the main things that hinder your ability to do a good job?

899. Is quality audit a prerequisite for program accreditation or program recognition?

900. Does the supplier use a formal quality system?

901. How does your organization know that its quality of teaching is appropriately effective and constructive?

902. How does your organization know that its risk management system is appropriately effective and constructive?

903. Are training programs documented?

904. Are there sufficient personnel having the necessary education, background, training, and experience to assure that all operations are correctly performed?

905. Have the risks associated with the intentions been identified, analyzed and appropriate responses developed?

906. What review processes are in place for your organizations major activities?

907. Are the review comments incorporated?

908. Are all areas associated with the storage and reconditioning of devices clean, free of rubbish, adequately ventilated and in good repair?

909. How does your organization know that its methods are appropriately effective and constructive?

910. Is there a written corporate quality policy?

3.6 Team Directory: Risks Dashboard

911. How do unidentified risks impact the outcome of the Risks Dashboard project?

912. Who are your stakeholders (customers, sponsors, end users, team members)?

913. Who should receive information (all stakeholders)?

914. Why is the work necessary?

915. Who are the Team Members?

916. Timing: when do the effects of communication take place?

917. Days from the time the issue is identified?

918. How will you accomplish and manage the objectives?

919. Decisions: is the most suitable form of contract being used?

920. Process decisions: how well was task order work performed?

921. Contract requirements complied with?

922. Process decisions: is work progressing on schedule and per contract requirements?

923. Do purchase specifications and configurations match requirements?

924. Who will be the stakeholders on your next Risks Dashboard project?

925. When will you produce deliverables?

926. Process decisions: do job conditions warrant additional actions to collect job information and document on-site activity?

927. When does information need to be distributed?

3.7 Team Operating Agreement: Risks Dashboard

928. Is compensation based on team and individual performance?

929. Do you post any action items, due dates, and responsibilities on the team website?

930. Do you record meetings for the already stated unable to attend?

931. How will you divide work equitably?

932. Are there more than two functional areas represented by your team?

933. Do you leverage technology engagement tools group chat, polls, screen sharing, etc.?

934. Did you delegate tasks such as taking meeting minutes, presenting a topic and soliciting input?

935. Do you listen for voice tone and word choice to understand the meaning behind words?

936. Resource allocation: how will individual team members account for time and expenses, and how will this be allocated in the team budget?

937. Did you recap the meeting purpose, time, and expectations?

938. Do you determine the meeting length and time of day?

939. Did you prepare participants for the next meeting?

940. What is culture?

941. Do you use a parking lot for any items that are important and outside of the agenda?

942. Have you set the goals and objectives of the team?

943. Are team roles clearly defined and accepted?

944. What is group supervision?

945. The method to be used in the decision making process; Will it be consensus, majority rule, or the supervisor having the final say?

946. Seconds for members to respond?

947. Are there the right people on your team?

3.8 Team Performance Assessment: Risks Dashboard

948. To what degree do team members agree with the goals, relative importance, and the ways in which achievement will be measured?

949. To what degree does the teams work approach provide opportunity for members to engage in open interaction?

950. To what degree will team members, individually and collectively, commit time to help themselves and others learn and develop skills?

951. What is method variance?

952. To what degree does the teams work approach provide opportunity for members to engage in results-based evaluation?

953. How hard did you try to make a good selection?

954. What structural changes have you made or are you preparing to make?

955. Individual task proficiency and team process behavior: what is important for team functioning?

956. Which situations call for a more extreme type of adaptiveness in which team members actually re-define roles?

957. To what degree do team members understand one anothers roles and skills?

958. To what degree are the skill areas critical to team performance present?

959. To what degree do team members feel that the purpose of the team is important, if not exciting?

960. To what degree does the teams approach to its work allow for modification and improvement over time?

961. What makes opportunities more or less obvious?

962. To what degree does the team possess adequate membership to achieve its ends?

963. Can team performance be reliably measured in simulator and live exercises using the same assessment tool?

964. Where to from here?

965. What are teams?

966. What are you doing specifically to develop the leaders around you?

967. To what degree do team members articulate the teams work approach?

3.9 Team Member Performance Assessment: Risks Dashboard

968. To what degree are sub-teams possible or necessary?

969. Do the goals support your organizations goals?

970. Why were corresponding selected?

971. What innovations (if any) are developed to realize goals?

972. To what degree are the goals ambitious?

973. What steps have you taken to improve performance?

974. Are the goals SMART ?

975. How do you use data to inform instruction and improve staff achievement?

976. What makes them effective?

977. What are top priorities?

978. What are they responsible for?

979. Is it clear how goals will be accomplished?

980. To what degree do team members frequently explore the teams purpose and its implications?

981. To what degree can all members engage in open and interactive considerations?

982. To what degree can team members meet frequently enough to accomplish the teams ends?

983. What qualities does a successful Team leader possess?

984. To what degree are the teams goals and objectives clear, simple, and measurable?

985. How do you implement Cost Reduction?

986. How do you determine which data are the most important to use, analyze, or review?

987. Did training work?

3.10 Issue Log: Risks Dashboard

988. Is there an important stakeholder who is actively opposed and will not receive messages?

989. What is the status of the issue?

990. Is access to the Issue Log controlled?

991. Who have you worked with in past, similar initiatives?

992. What steps can you take for positive relationships?

993. How is this initiative related to other portfolios, programs, or Risks Dashboard projects?

994. Why do you manage communications?

995. How were past initiatives successful?

996. Are stakeholder roles recognized by your organization?

997. What are the stakeholders interrelationships?

998. What effort will a change need?

999. Is the issue log kept in a safe place?

1000. In classifying stakeholders, which approach to do so are you using?

1001. What would have to change?

1002. Are you constantly rushing from meeting to meeting?

1003. Which stakeholders are thought leaders, influences, or early adopters?

4.0 Monitoring and Controlling Process Group: Risks Dashboard

1004. Did it work?

1005. Is the verbiage used appropriate and understandable?

1006. Is it what was agreed upon?

1007. How is agile Risks Dashboard project management done?

1008. Is there adequate validation on required fields?

1009. Where is the Risk in the Risks Dashboard project?

1010. Just how important is your work to the overall success of the Risks Dashboard project?

1011. What resources (both financial and non-financial) are available/needed?

1012. Does the solution fit in with organizations technical architectural requirements?

1013. How were collaborations developed, and how are they sustained?

1014. What factors are contributing to progress or delay in the achievement of products and results?

1015. When will the Risks Dashboard project be done?

1016. How well did the chosen processes produce the expected results?

1017. If action is called for, what form should it take?

1018. Who are the Risks Dashboard project stakeholders?

1019. Were sponsors and decision makers available when needed outside regularly scheduled meetings?

1020. Overall, how does the program function to serve the clients?

1021. What resources are necessary?

4.1 Project Performance Report: Risks Dashboard

1022. To what degree do all members feel responsible for all agreed-upon measures?

1023. What is the degree to which rules govern information exchange between groups?

1024. To what degree does the informal organization make use of individual resources and meet individual needs?

1025. To what degree does the information network communicate information relevant to the task?

1026. To what degree will new and supplemental skills be introduced as the need is recognized?

1027. To what degree will each member have the opportunity to advance his or her professional skills in all three of the above categories while contributing to the accomplishment of the teams purpose and goals?

1028. Next Steps?

1029. To what degree do the relationships of the informal organization motivate taskrelevant behavior and facilitate task completion?

1030. To what degree can the cognitive capacity of individuals accommodate the flow of information?

1031. To what degree are the members clear on what they are individually responsible for and what they are jointly responsible for?

1032. To what degree are the goals realistic?

1033. How is the data used?

1034. To what degree are the demands of the task compatible with and converge with the relationships of the informal organization?

1035. To what degree does the teams work approach provide opportunity for members to engage in fact-based problem solving?

1036. To what degree do members articulate the goals beyond the team membership?

4.2 Variance Analysis: Risks Dashboard

1037. Are authorized changes being incorporated in a timely manner?

1038. The anticipated business volume?

1039. Historical experience?

1040. Are overhead costs budgets established on a basis consistent with the anticipated direct business base?

1041. How have the setting and use of standards changed over time?

1042. Do the rates and prices remain constant throughout the year?

1043. Why are standard cost systems used?

1044. Did a new competitor enter the market?

1045. How does the monthly budget compare to the actual experience?

1046. Does the contractor use objective results, design reviews and tests to trace schedule performance?

1047. What is the performance to date and material commitment?

1048. Are control accounts opened and closed based on the start and completion of work contained therein?

1049. Contract line items and end items?

1050. How are material, labor, and overhead variances calculated and recorded?

1051. Is budgeted cost for work performed calculated in a manner consistent with the way work is planned?

1052. Are data elements reconcilable between internal summary reports and reports forwarded to the stakeholders?

1053. What is exceptional?

1054. Are all budgets assigned to control accounts?

1055. What can be the cause of an increase in costs?

4.3 Earned Value Status: Risks Dashboard

1056. Earned value can be used in almost any Risks Dashboard project situation and in almost any Risks Dashboard project environment. it may be used on large Risks Dashboard projects, medium sized Risks Dashboard projects, tiny Risks Dashboard projects (in cut-down form), complex and simple Risks Dashboard projects and in any market sector. some people, of course, know all about earned value, they have used it for years - but perhaps not as effectively as they could have?

1057. When is it going to finish?

1058. How does this compare with other Risks Dashboard projects?

1059. Where are your problem areas?

1060. Validation is a process of ensuring that the developed system will actually achieve the stakeholders desired outcomes; Are you building the right product? What do you validate?

1061. Are you hitting your Risks Dashboard projects targets?

1062. Verification is a process of ensuring that the developed system satisfies the stakeholders agreements and specifications; Are you building the product right? What do you verify?

1063. If earned value management (EVM) is so good in determining the true status of a Risks Dashboard project and Risks Dashboard project its completion, why is it that hardly any one uses it in information systems related Risks Dashboard projects?

1064. How much is it going to cost by the finish?

1065. Where is evidence-based earned value in your organization reported?

1066. What is the unit of forecast value?

4.4 Risk Audit: Risks Dashboard

1067. How do you govern assets?

1068. Is the auditor able to evaluate contradictory evidence in an unbiased manner?

1069. Have risks been considered with an insurance broker or provider and suitable insurance cover been arranged?

1070. Do you meet the legislative requirements (for example PAYG, super contributions) for paid employees?

1071. Estimated size of product in number of programs, files, transactions?

1072. What expertise does the Board have on quality, outcomes, and errors?

1073. What limitations do auditors face in effectively applying risk-assessment results to the risk of material misstatement measures?

1074. Does your organization have an up-to-date constitution?

1075. Tradeoff: how much risk can be tolerated and still deliver the products where they need to be?

1076. Why do audits fail?

1077. How do you prioritize risks?

1078. Are all managers or operators of the facility or equipment competent or qualified?

1079. Are policies communicated to all affected?

1080. Is safety information provided to all involved?

1081. Are risk management strategies documented?

1082. Are end-users enthusiastically committed to the Risks Dashboard project and the system/product to be built?

1083. Will an appropriate standard of care be applied to all involved?

1084. Does your auditor understand your business?

1085. Have you considered the health and safety of everyone in your organization and do you meet work health and safety regulations?

4.5 Contractor Status Report: Risks Dashboard

1086. What is the average response time for answering a support call?

1087. How is risk transferred?

1088. What process manages the contracts?

1089. Describe how often regular updates are made to the proposed solution. Are corresponding regular updates included in the standard maintenance plan?

1090. How long have you been using the services?

1091. What was the overall budget or estimated cost?

1092. What are the minimum and optimal bandwidth requirements for the proposed solution?

1093. Are there contractual transfer concerns?

1094. What was the final actual cost?

1095. What was the budget or estimated cost for your organizations services?

1096. What was the actual budget or estimated cost for your organizations services?

1097. How does the proposed individual meet each requirement?

1098. If applicable; describe your standard schedule for new software version releases. Are new software version releases included in the standard maintenance plan?

1099. Who can list a Risks Dashboard project as organization experience, your organization or a previous employee of your organization?

4.6 Formal Acceptance: Risks Dashboard

1100. Does it do what Risks Dashboard project team said it would?

1101. Have all comments been addressed?

1102. Do you buy pre-configured systems or build your own configuration?

1103. What can you do better next time?

1104. How well did the team follow the methodology?

1105. Who supplies data?

1106. What are the requirements against which to test, Who will execute?

1107. Was the Risks Dashboard project work done on time, within budget, and according to specification?

1108. Did the Risks Dashboard project achieve its MOV?

1109. General estimate of the costs and times to complete the Risks Dashboard project?

1110. What is the Acceptance Management Process?

1111. Do you perform formal acceptance or burn-in tests?

1112. Was the client satisfied with the Risks Dashboard project results?

1113. How does your team plan to obtain formal acceptance on your Risks Dashboard project?

1114. Was the Risks Dashboard project goal achieved?

1115. Was the sponsor/customer satisfied?

1116. Does it do what client said it would?

1117. Did the Risks Dashboard project manager and team act in a professional and ethical manner?

1118. What lessons were learned about your Risks Dashboard project management methodology?

1119. Do you buy-in installation services?

5.0 Closing Process Group: Risks Dashboard

1120. Will the Risks Dashboard project deliverable(s) replace a current asset or group of assets?

1121. Who are the Risks Dashboard project stakeholders?

1122. What is the overall risk of the Risks Dashboard project to your organization?

1123. Did you do what you said you were going to do?

1124. Did the Risks Dashboard project team have the right skills?

1125. Was the schedule met?

1126. What areas does the group agree are the biggest success on the Risks Dashboard project?

1127. Is there a clear cause and effect between the activity and the lesson learned?

1128. What were the desired outcomes?

1129. What is the risk of failure to your organization?

1130. How will you do it?

1131. Are there funding or time constraints?

1132. Were cost budgets met?

1133. What could be done to improve the process?

1134. What is the Risks Dashboard project Management Process?

1135. Based on your Risks Dashboard project communication management plan, what worked well?

5.1 Procurement Audit: Risks Dashboard

1136. Were standards, certifications and evidence required admissible?

1137. Were no tenders presented after the time limit accepted?

1138. Where required, were candidates registered as approved contractors, suppliers or service providers or certified by relevant bodies?

1139. Are procurement policies and practices in line with (international) good practice standards?

1140. Are there policies regarding special approval for capital expenditures?

1141. Are services/tasks combined in such a way that the market is used where relevant?

1142. Can changes be made to automatic disbursement programs without proper approval of management?

1143. Do established procedures ensure that computer programs will not pay the same group of invoices twice?

1144. Is there a form specified for bids?

1145. Is there no evidence of collusion between

bidders?

1146. Is confidentiality guaranteed during the whole process?

1147. Is there a policy covering the relationship of other departments with vendors?

1148. Are the users needs clearly and invariably defined and has the expected outcome or mission been clearly identified and communicated in measurable terms?

1149. Is the performance of the procurement function/unit benchmarked with other procurement functions/units in the different stages of the procurement process?

1150. Does the contract meet criteria of completeness and consistency?

1151. Is the opportunity properly published?

1152. Is the purchasing department responsible for a continual review of marketing trends, particularly on long-term contracts and contracts containing escalation clauses?

1153. Are there procedures governing the negotiations of long-term contracts?

1154. Are approvals needed if changes are made in the quantity or specification of the original purchase requisition?

1155. Does the procurement function/unit

understand costumer needs, supply markets and suppliers?

5.2 Contract Close-Out: Risks Dashboard

1156. Change in knowledge?

1157. Have all contracts been closed?

1158. Has each contract been audited to verify acceptance and delivery?

1159. Was the contract complete without requiring numerous changes and revisions?

1160. Parties: Authorized?

1161. Have all contracts been completed?

1162. What is capture management?

1163. What happens to the recipient of services?

1164. Have all contract records been included in the Risks Dashboard project archives?

1165. How does it work?

1166. Have all acceptance criteria been met prior to final payment to contractors?

1167. Are the signers the authorized officials?

1168. Parties: who is involved?

1169. How is the contracting office notified of the automatic contract close-out?

1170. Was the contract type appropriate?

1171. Change in attitude or behavior?

1172. How/when used ?

1173. Change in circumstances?

1174. Was the contract sufficiently clear so as not to result in numerous disputes and misunderstandings?

1175. Why Outsource?

5.3 Project or Phase Close-Out: Risks Dashboard

1176. If you were the Risks Dashboard project sponsor, how would you determine which Risks Dashboard project team(s) and/or individuals deserve recognition?

1177. Who controlled the resources for the Risks Dashboard project?

1178. How often did each stakeholder need an update?

1179. Which changes might a stakeholder be required to make as a result of the Risks Dashboard project?

1180. What was expected from each stakeholder?

1181. What were the actual outcomes?

1182. What information is each stakeholder group interested in?

1183. Does the lesson describe a function that would be done differently the next time?

1184. How much influence did the stakeholder have over others?

1185. Does the lesson educate others to improve performance?

1186. What is the information level of detail required for each stakeholder?

1187. Were risks identified and mitigated?

1188. Were messages directly related to the release strategy or phases of the Risks Dashboard project?

1189. What is in it for you?

1190. What were the goals and objectives of the communications strategy for the Risks Dashboard project?

1191. Who exerted influence that has positively affected or negatively impacted the Risks Dashboard project?

1192. What was learned?

1193. What can you do better next time, and what specific actions can you take to improve?

1194. What are the mandatory communication needs for each stakeholder?

5.4 Lessons Learned: Risks Dashboard

1195. Did the Risks Dashboard project management methodology work?

1196. What were the key issues?

1197. How was the political and social history changed over the life of the Risks Dashboard project?

1198. What solutions or recommendations can you offer that would have improved some aspect of the Risks Dashboard project?

1199. How did the estimated Risks Dashboard project Budget compare with the total actual expenditures?

1200. What are the skills directly related to the task?

1201. What are the expectations of the individuals?

1202. What was the methodology behind successful learning experiences, and how might they be applied to the broader challenge of your organizations knowledge management?

1203. What data are likely to be missing?

1204. Are there any hidden conflicts of interest?

1205. What are your lessons learned that you will keep in mind for the next Risks Dashboard project you participate in?

1206. How effective was the quality assurance process?

1207. Was the Risks Dashboard project significantly delayed/hampered by outside dependencies (outside to the Risks Dashboard project, that is)?

1208. What things mattered the most on this Risks Dashboard project?

1209. Who needs to learn lessons?

1210. What is the growth stage of your organization?

1211. Would you spend your own time fixing this issue?

1212. What are the influence patterns?

1213. Under what legal authority did your organization head and program manager direct your organization and Risks Dashboard project?

1214. What are the needs of the individuals?

Index

279

prices 236
primary   48, 126, 163
principles   132, 189
priorities   43, 49-51, 54, 208, 228
prioritize   198, 240
priority 42, 49, 155
privacy   31
probably   162
problem   15, 17-18, 20-22, 26, 28, 36-38, 51, 65, 212, 219,
235, 238
problems   18-19, 21-23, 72, 82, 85, 97, 130, 182
procedure   214
procedures   9, 76, 88, 92, 95, 144, 150, 160, 170, 178, 180, 208,
218, 248-249
proceed   192
proceeding   167
process   1-7, 9, 28, 31, 33, 35-37, 40-41, 57, 59-61, 63-64,
66-69, 72, 74, 87-88, 90-92, 94, 96-98, 123, 130, 132, 134-135, 137,
139-140, 142-144, 150-151, 160, 164-165, 167, 178-179, 182-183,
188, 192, 196, 198, 207, 210, 218, 222-223, 225-226, 232, 238, 242,
244, 246-247, 249, 256
processes   43, 45, 57-59, 61-62, 65-68, 89, 94, 96, 123, 134,
145, 178, 193, 216, 220-221, 233
procuring   210
produce   65, 160, 213, 223, 233
produced   69, 74, 131
producing   140
product   1, 53, 58, 63, 103, 130, 137, 142-143, 145, 156,
168, 176, 179, 196, 200, 211, 213, 238, 240-241
production   74, 102
products   1, 21, 23, 44, 101, 108, 130-131, 141, 149, 176,
193, 210, 212, 232, 240
profile 220
program   16, 47, 61, 96, 123, 130, 186, 195, 220, 233, 256
programme   131
programs   133, 212, 220-221, 230, 240, 248
progress   37, 43, 84, 91, 111, 150, 174, 182-183, 232
prohibited   148
project 2-8, 17, 21, 25, 29, 47, 68, 70, 92, 94, 96, 100, 102, 105,
112, 114, 116-118, 122-128, 130-140, 142-147, 150-156, 158-159,
162-174, 176-178, 184-185, 187-188, 190-192, 195, 197-199, 202-
203, 206-207, 210-214, 216, 222-223, 232-234, 238-239, 241, 243-
247, 251, 253-256

required   23, 26, 28, 32, 40, 42, 67-68, 75, 77, 82, 92, 134, 145, 152, 154-155, 165, 167, 180, 194, 206, 208, 232, 248, 253-254
requiring   127, 251
research   24, 104, 156, 165, 220
reserved   1
reserves   149
reside 73
resolution   58, 78, 191
resolve 16, 23
resolved   171-172, 180, 192, 210
Resource   3-4, 109, 134, 160, 162-163, 165, 188, 213, 224
resources   2, 7, 17, 22, 24, 30, 32, 45, 70, 75, 77, 92, 95, 98, 102, 109, 113, 120, 124, 128-129, 152, 154-155, 158, 162, 170, 172, 174, 189, 202, 206, 232-234, 253
respect   1
respective   130
respond   131, 225
responded   11
responding   195
response   16, 24, 91, 95, 97, 242
responses   106, 194-195, 198, 221
responsive   166, 174
result 74, 85, 130, 142-143, 149, 173-174, 176, 181, 216, 252-253
resulted   91
resulting   64, 142
results 8, 33, 39, 59, 71, 77, 79-80, 84-85, 92-93, 130-132, 154, 174, 178, 180, 232-233, 236, 240, 245
Retain 99
retained   63
retention   50
retrospect   111
return 74, 107, 182, 198
returns 198
revenue   25, 52
revenues   48
review 9, 67, 207, 219, 221, 229, 249
reviewed   35, 144, 195
reviews143, 150, 178, 196-197, 206, 236
revised 68, 91
revisions   251
reward 44, 47, 212
rewarded   20
rewards   89

Made in the USA
Middletown, DE
02 September 2021